Uncommon
REMEDIES
FOR AMERICA'S ILLS
futuring for the new millennium

D1521142

John F. McGrew, Ed.D.

NEW VISTA PRESS

Uncommon Remedies for America's Ills:
Futuring for the New Millennium

by John F. McGrew, Ed.D.

Published by:
NEW VISTA PRESS
P.O. Box 3554
Ashland, Oregon 97520

Copyright © 1997 by John F. McGrew

Cover and book design by Jonah Bornstein, Wellstone Publications

Publisher's Cataloging in Publication Data
McGrew, John Ferris
    Uncommon remedies for America's Ills
    Includes Index
    1. Current Affairs
    2. Futurism
    3. Influencing Politics

I. McGrew, John F. 1928–
(JK 1118) MI 309.262   96-92648
ISBN 0-936544-08-2

Contents

DEDICATION

My normal inclination would be to skip a dedication page. Such pages are often unduly mysterious or a bit gushy. My third grade teacher inspired me, but her incorporation into a dedication would be a stretch; likewise my old scoutmaster. Better would have been the seventeen year old junior assistant scout leader, for at Boy Scout camp he made an effort to give us some post taps discourses on sex education. When you are bumbling into puberty and have no sisters, such instruction is important. It was more than the information, for most of that was wrong. It was a timely concept. At least Dedications enable writers to look back and contemplate where inspiration is conceived.

For parents. Basically I am thinking of my own for they engendered in me the belief that one does not have to join the world at a lock step pace. They enabled me to dream and seriously challenge traditional "whys" as to how things happen and what things should happen. However, I will go a major leap beyond and recognize all parents as a vital part of our civilization. The fact that so many are doing it badly is not a good sign for the pending millennium. This book will take a long look at parents and their "bewildering offspring".

To the women in my life! Mom has been mentioned so let's enter two former wives, two daughters and two granddaughters, friends, the "thoughtful and perceptive buddy" group, and those for whom I felt a special passion.

To the men (this completes covering the sexes)! My father, a son, four grandsons, friends, comrades and confidantes.

To my high school and college classmates. No one really deserves to be encompassed into such decent groups of people. This could be called "the luck of the draw".

To Charles Dickens. He gave us a man named Micawber and the simple belief that spending more money than one person (or one government) earns will precipitate a problem.

To a man named William Shakespeare. He proved that one person in one lifetime can promote universal ideas that subsequently influenced mankind over the centuries. In one brief passage in *Hamlet* he noted for all to observe that we should "Neither a borrower nor a lender be" and "This above all to thine own self be true and it must follow as the night the day, thou canst not then be false to any man".

To certain "down to earth" people who have impacted our society with an infusion of a vital ingredient, "common sense". My group would include but not be limited to Ann Landers and her sister Abby (fellow Iowans), Oprah Winfrey, Dr. Robert Schuller, Dr. Joyce Brothers, Larry King; listened to folks with very different backgrounds who dispense in a few syllables ideas that make sense.

To Maylon Drake and a host of other educators who have paced my chosen profession of education. This book constantly points out that if changes are to be made in our society on the threshold of the new millennium, the schools, the common denominator in our lives, have a critical role to play.

To a carpenter from Nazareth who has inspired a large part of mankind for two millennia with the simplest rule, "Love thy neighbor as thyself". When we realize the ongoing truth of Jon Donne's "No man is an island", we will know that some form of faith is essential for the well being of man. We may never truly understand that force behind nature, the "why?" factor, but introspection and meditation allow a calmness and hopefully reason to enter otherwise busy and confused lives.

To my children and grandchildren, already mentioned but to be reemphasized, for them and their progeny and countless others like them, the new millennium will be a reality. It is incumbent on those of us who are bridging the change of centuries and start of the new millennium to leave a legacy of reason and, when possible, resolution of those ills which face our nation and all nations.

INTRODUCTION

*W*hat better time than the threshold of the 21st Century to ruminate on history and make forecasts for the future. Unique problems face the nation and the world; yet unusual situations have always bedeviled mankind and dinosaurkind before homo sapiens. Prophets of doom and gloom have predicted at the least woe and even the big blast, Armageddon itself as "hull up on the horizon" from time immemorial. A stronger challenge is to project light at the end of the tunnel, to promote an optimistic forecast for many tomorrows, and to suggest that there are remedies to many of the annoyances of the era. Such is the nature of this book.

Charles Dickens commenced the immortal *Tale of Two Cities* with the projection that it was the best of times and the worst of times. We may still consider such a statement valid today. Incidentally Dickens through his novel *David Copperfield* also gave us a prescription for one of the simple solutions to be encompassed in this enterprise. If an entity, be it a person or a government, spends less than it earns, the results will be positive.

The United States has emerged in its 220 years since the Declaration of Independence from the new kid on the block to preeminent nation in the world. This is not necessarily a goal we have sought, and geography and time have insulated us from major catastrophes that have propelled history. The responsibility is awesome, and as we look at the 21st century, our house is not in the best order possible. It would not be difficult for us to climb back into our cocoon as one approach to facing seemingly insurmountable world problems, but technology has largely removed distance and time, our historic safeguards.

Sobering news is handed us daily. We are reminded that the younger generation for the first time in our history may not achieve the standard of living that their parents have enjoyed. There are terribly divisive issues in the land from the trauma of abortion, to gun control, and the issue of guaranteed rights for minorities including women (a misstatement since females outnumber males), various races and gays. Contemporary morality in the United States is under indictment as illegitimacy flourishes, drug use is rampant, crime surges upward, and communicable diseases seem to threaten everyone. Divorce and single parents approach the rule, rather than the exception.Quo vadis?

Remedies to our major problems avoid consensus and defeat the best minds in the land, most of which are still attached to humans who have the added pressure of necessarily being "politically correct" in an era where this may be impossible. It has been said to find an answer to an economic quandary, seek consensus from six top ranking economists and you will emerge with ten solutions. Perhaps the erudite, the expert, the specialists try too hard. Therefore presented herewith is a layman's guide for remedies for ranking national issues.

This writer may be categorized as a mainstream American citizen. There are footholds of experience from which projected remedies for problems may stem. Beyond the pale of reading, listening, observing and thinking, there have been other opportunities to formulate ideas. My status as militarist stems from being the 22,000th graduate of the U.S. Naval Academy transferred to the Air Force with Far East duty during the Korean War (which apparently was the armed conflict with inadequate status to enable us to develop our own post war syndrome a la Vietnam). Upon receiving a temporary physical disability discharge, I entered a thirty year teaching and school administrative career. As a high school principal in Southern California, I became one of a select group to have our own campus race riots.

I have always had an interest in history, and the written word intrigues me. My doctoral dissertation at USC won an award for being the most boring statement that year (a self appointed honor, actually). My interest in financial planning was aggrandized through the College for Financial Planning (CFP) program, and my concern for the law was heightened by being a victim of the legal system through a spurious slander suit. At one point I was an erstwhile politician having been involved in a congressional campaign and two school office tries with a perfect record . . . no victories. Like most, I pay taxes and have a viewpoint, and I have been a small businessman in the areas of real estate, insurance, travel, and publishing. I consider myself a religious person who talks to God through prayer, but I would be less than honest (unlike some of the charismatic religious leaders) to state that God has involved me in direct, two way conversations. The good news is that I am not running for office nor am I particularly anxious to be politically correct. My goal is not to consciously offend readers, but sometimes disagreement can stimulate the brain cells.

A few caveats. People should be responsible for their

actions and must largely solve their own problems. The corollary is that we often are not and some times cannot. There is probably no substitute for common sense.

In recent years we have seen a heightening of citizen reaction to their concerns about government. The initiative process is alive and well in America. In fact, judging from the number of propositions on many ballots to effect change, the point of overkill may be approaching. What is impressive is to note that a citizen with an idea can make a big difference, and a group of activists can move political mountains.

My hope is to precipitate a reaction on the part of the reader. Please disagree with me often; otherwise, I will have failed as I present this occasionally tongue in cheek guide for remedying our nation's woes as we enter the 21st century and another millennium.

CHAPTER 1
LICENSING THE BIRTHRIGHT

*W*hat would you think of a remedy which would practically eliminate abortions, markedly control money spent on Aid for Dependent Children (AFDC), stop illegitimacy, reduce crime, and radically lower the number of children living in poverty?

One would have to be a total recluse not to comprehend the magnitude of the problem of abortions in the United States. This year notwithstanding the era of the pill and other sophisticated birth control devices, almost a million and a half abortions will be performed. The ongoing conflict between "pro-choice" and "pro-life" forces is a national disgrace. Billions of dollars are being spent on AFDC, and illegitimacies run rampant. Seven out of ten black children are born out of wedlock and three of ten white births are illegitimate. Needless to say, the number of children living under the poverty level is burgeoning.

With increasing poverty levels and a lack of positive, responsible father figures, a high proportion of future criminals are being produced, primarily in the inner cities.

Being judgmental is not my goal. Perhaps our citizens

could agree on moral problems, but we would have difficulty defining solutions under contemporary rules, let alone in implementing remedies. Yet an ostensibly radical remedy might work. How about licensing the right to have children?

Americans are familiar with obtaining licenses for such mundane things as cars and dogs. A closer parallel might be the marrriage license where we must meet requirements of minimum age, residency, and often procure a health clearance. Could we agree that a couple, prior to having a baby, should be married (perhaps for a minimum amount of time such as six months or a year), have a home (four walls and a roof above), a source of income, and perhaps even post a bond of say $5,000 to insure a diaper supply and baby food for a year? This fee would represent less than half the cost of a low priced car.

Non controversial so far? (Okay, Okay. I may have ruffled the feathers of some homosexual couples, ostensibly well qualified single would be parents, a few Hollywood types who just want to have a baby for the hell of it, and other couples who share space but do not want to be married. We can negotiate. Sorry for the lapse since I promised to be non-judgmental).

Comes the concomitant harder part! All Americans must be willing to go on a birth control system. Solution "Y" would be placed in all liquids we imbibe; something like fluoridating water. Males will also participate to be fair (and offset a feminist concern). Scientists, of course, will have a major challenge to produce such a panacea, the aforementioned Solution " Y", which will have no or extremely minimal side effects. It would be helpful if the material also contained vitamin C and helps cure the common cold. By the way, the scientist developing Solution "Y" would be making a great leap toward a Nobel Prize .

I am in my sixties, already neutered by a vasectomy,

but I will still volunteer to take the first dose of the concoction.

Another task for scientists is to develop Antidote "Z" that would offset the birth control material. This would be made available to those who are licensed to have children. The fee for the baby license, perhaps several hundred dollars, would cover costs.

Let's minimize "big brother". Licensing connotes some state control, but we shall scratch any clever rules such as IQ testing, congenital limitations, citizenship requirements, number of children per family, racial quotas or whatever.

The first major advantage of such "baby licensing" would be the practical elimination of the need for abortions. Doctors performing legal abortions have been assaulted in growing numbers in recent years and seek relief through new laws to give them greater protection. Pro-lifers, many of whom claim to be fundamentalist Christians, increasingly use un-Christian tactics including murder to further their goals. A hidden variable in the drama must be the trauma that is locked in the heart and soul of every woman who has had an abortion, and this will persist for their lifetime. Let's eliminate the need!

There also is genuine concern among political partisans that the issue of abortion may mortally fragment the Republican Party.

A problem which may not be solved through my proposal; indeed, it could be exacerbated, would be that of disease. AIDS and other sexually transmitted diseases which may be minimized through the use of condoms could be expanded if the birth control use of condoms was rendered unnecessary. Of course, condoms could still be utilized for "safe sex", if there is such a thing. The rupture rate of condoms is relatively high, something akin to the odds in Russian roulette.

How about the practical elimination of much welfare?

The cost for AFDC continues to mount often becoming not only a lifetime welfare ticket, but also a multi-generational problem. The most recent figure I have seen on illegitimacy is 26 percent of all American births. A valid question remains whether AFDC encourages young people who seemingly face a hopelessly sterile existence (not in terms of sexuality but in terms of poverty and culture) to become pregnant after which they will suddenly have money given to them. A continuing life of poverty and cultural deprivation is almost assured along with the difficult challenge of raising a child and too often, more children.

A major problem for the system of licensing children can be seen with religious extremists who oppose birth control. Many of these people are militant "pro-lifers" so the "licensing" plan which would eliminate abortions would represent a serious conflict of interests regarding birth control. Fortunately the fall of the Soviet empire will have eliminated those who saw "fluoridation" of drinking water as a communist conspiracy. Fluorides have resulted in a new generation of children with strong teeth.

Another major plus for my proposal would be the reduction of staggering medical costs, not only those related to abortion, but also attending the medical needs of children born to "crack" mothers and others born into poverty. Certainly blood testing required in many states for marriage and potentially applied to licensing birth would go a long way to reducing the number of children born with AIDS and other diseases.

I will not dwell on the challenge of developing the necessary birth control material, solutions "Y" and "Z", although it is a critical variable. First we need a national will and the way might follow, led by those who placed men on the moon and virtually eliminated polio and rubella.

Now for an editorial comment on sexual activity for

children— call it judgmental, wishful thinking, or reminiscent of years gone by. In my bucolic high school and college days BP (Before the Pill), by and large "good girls didn't" and the guys accepted that. Life was probably infinitely simpler then. There is a remote chance that contemporary teenagers, seeing the problems inherent if not epidemic in their generation, could mount an abstinence challenge with the same positive level of success of their grass roots inspired SADD (Students Against Driving Drunk) and "Just Say No (to drugs)" campaigns.

Meanwhile how about a "baby license? Could it possibly sell?

CHAPTER 2
EDUCATION RUN AMOK

*M*ost Americans believe that our schools are an extremely important part of our nation's heart beat. Yet there is frustration throughout the land as the media point out declining achievement scores and gang activity spreading to the campus. Support levels are suffering from benign neglect. Everyone has an opinion of what can be done to rectify the contemporary educational scene, but preponderantly solutions are oriented to throwing more money at the status quo. The solution is not that complex, but it would take collective determination on the part of educators, parents, the community, and above all else, the clients themselves, the school children. Therein rests much of the problem.

Put me down on the side of the angels. As an educator, teacher and administrator for over thirty years the scene has intrigued me. Historically as public education has developed so has the nation flourished. The United States has genuinely committed itself to educating its youth. At one recent point no nation in the world was able to place over 17 percent of its young people to the equivalent of the American High School graduate. Most nations had caste systems whereby masses of their students after a rudimentary education went directly into the work force. Other nations have an elitist class system with emphasis on private schools.

So what is the problem? Why all the criticism in contemporary times? Our top students may be better educated than ever before, but the masses of our students are suffering from terminal softness. Naturally anyone even reasonably associated with education swears allegiance to the three Rs. I am more concerned over the three As which have led to a major muck up of the educational process in recent years, recent being defined as the past fifty years or since the advent of the "baby boomers". Now we are back to my era so perhaps I am personally responsible, and candidly, I am sure I have been part of the problem.

The three As are AFFLUENCE, APATHY, AND ADVERSITY (or lack thereof). I remember when I first started teaching in the fifties, the GIs had come home after World War II and their kids were flooding into the schools. They had lived through the depression and then slogged through the morass of combat, resolving along the way that when they came home and had a family, their kids would have it better. So a give away program started for many. The period of affluence, the first A, had begun "Don't earn it; just take it!" There was little of that third A or adversity to contend with; the mettle of the young was not being tested. Of course, there were many exceptions, but even looking at today's scene, who are blazing the academic trail in the United States? The boat people who came through hell in South East Asia are working diligently in their roles in this new land be it on the job or in the school. As a matter of fact, one major task is to instill in young people that school is their job—the number one task in their lives.

Which leads to the second A or APATHY. Recent informal surveys of high school students reveal that their education is far down their list of priorities. More important are dates, sports, cars, jobs, clothing, being "cool", music and entertainment. Schools are boring, teachers dull and uninspiring, academics are irrelevant. Who needs it? Of course, the modern "kids" are getting their three squares a day, the laundry is done, new clothing magically appears of the right label, often a car is delivered when one is old enough to drive, little if any work is required around the house, and Mom especially, perhaps the only parent, but at least a working parent has more than a little guilt feeling about her role, so "give away" is the game. No one said the kids are basically dumb. (The word may be "lazy", but not dumb). Why not accept such a "deal"?

Two other major impacts have further thrown education off kilter in the past thirty years. Television has developed a life of its own preempting reading, studying, exercise, meetings, discussion, even rational family dining. Statistics now show that something over fifty percent of our citizens eat in front of the TV set. Certainly there are some positive points to be said for aspects of television, but Minnow's reference to a vast wasteland should be analyzed carefully. We may have become a land of entertainment freaks! Hand in hand with this technological miracle goes rock and roll. Just over thirty years ago the Beatles arrived on the scene. Now they would be considered staid and subdued, relatively, but they gave impetus to an industry and a monster. Combine the two and one winds up with Music TV

How can Wordsworth and Shakespeare possibly compete?

There has always been some disagreement as to the goal for education. This is especially true at the college level when education for the sake of education clashes with career training. Most responsible Americans would probably agree that students should develop some values and goals in school. They should be mindful that our society is work oriented, and a career must develop somewhere short of being an early committed member of the welfare force. One must function, pay bills and taxes, vote intelligently, become a responsible citizen, but a richer life in terms of the arts, literature, awareness of the world with its possibilities for travel and adventure is also a realistic goal for an educated person.

Strong proponents for work experience and technical training abound, and some feel that a student could emerge from high school with a salable skill that would enable a graduate to proceed directly into the work force or be able to support him or herself while pursuing higher education. This makes sense and strengthens the viewpoint that high school should be looked upon as a job. Labor unions, however, project another step of reality into the process. They say make sure students are well grounded in their basics, can read, write and do basic math, and the unions will place them in apprentice programs where they can learn a skill. Values and attitudes must also be part of the educational experience although most of these are engendered in the home.

I shall never forget the year that a telephone company rep came to our high school campus to speak to the work experience students. Her message was a powerful one and directly from the combat zone of real life experience. "We can test you to see whether you have picked up your basic three Rs, but the one thing we insist on knowing is your attendance record, for if you cut school regularly, you will not be the kind of employee we want."

Compulsory education is a mixed bag. For many years it protected youngsters and helped end horrible child labor practices. Now it often encourages a bad attitude on the part of students who feel they are forced to be where they do not want to be. We value higher something for which we must work, not necessarily something that is jammed upon us. In effect the schools have become a vast "holding tank" for young people to keep them from pursuing jobs, to keep them off the streets and potentially out of trouble, and to keep them safe. "Out of trouble" and "safe" are terms that often do not apply to the contemporary school environment, for modern problems have barged right on to school campuses and even into the classrooms.

Summer vacation is another idea whose time has passed by. Predictably there is some correlation with the amount of time on task and the outcome. The American school day and year is markedly shorter than those of many other students across the world which necessarily places us at a disadvantage. Far more significant is how the time is utilized in our schools and the seriousness of purpose with which our students face their job of schoolwork. Not every teacher is a born entertainer or marvelous motivator, but the attitude of "go ahead and teach me, teach!" with the corollary of "and I'll be resisting with every sinew" too often prevails. Using time well, concentration, applied study, competing with oneself, and saying "no" to interruptions and distractions are vital facets of self education today. Self-education is what it is all about. The old adage about leading a horse to water represents the truth. The teachers can push bodies up to the stream , but imbibing in the elixir of learning must be up to the student.

In my high school in Iowa a quotation had been painted over the proscenium arch in our auditorium. It was attributed to Shakespeare, but in later years when I tried to nail down the source and could not find it, I thought it might have been the brain child of an inspired sign painter. Later a more competent reference person informed me that it was from Act One , Scene Five of *Twelfth Night*, and when I read the passage in context it was not really the message I wanted. Simply stated it is, "WE WILL

DRAW THE CURTAIN AND SHOW YOU THE PICTURE."
My message from that quote is that the schools can draw
the curtain and show us what "might be" in our educational program, but as students we must make it happen
ourselves.

Another stuffy reality of American public education is
that it is coed, and I honestly believe that education seg-
regated by sex is best. In effect when half the audience is
playing to the other half based on some primitive glan-
dular instinct, the product loses. It is best we accept the
reality of coed education with the gain of a better social-
izing experience and let it go.

I do have trouble with the contemporary mishmash of
teacher discriminating against girls in the classroom and
in favor of boys. One must have a perverted agenda to
force this thought process through. Boys seem more generally distracted with other interests, and girls in school
and probably on the job are far better organized. Conceivably at some point historically girls were spending
energy not appearing too smart in some classrooms in
an effort to lure males, and they may not have been motivated by a more elusive goal of higher education and a
career. Surely now we have proceeded past that point,
and the motivation for women is at least as strong as for
males and even more so in a catch-up mode.

Unfortunately, there is a disclaimer. The "Cinderella"
or "mother's knee" syndrome still haunts me somewhat. In my later years in the classroom and well into
the era of the modern woman, my female high school
students generally accepted the fact that they were responsible for themselves and their careers. Occasionally one would confess that she was still waiting for
that Prince Charming to come and take her away from
her mundane worries.

We have made an innate assumption that all people
want to be educated, and at some level that might be

true. Formal academic education and life education with its heavy base in common sense are not always working in tandem. Our current youth are undoubtedly aware of the fact that for the first time in American history they may not achieve a life style sustained by their parents. It was easy for me to receive more education than my mother who did not finish high school. I was also able to pass my father's basic college degree with advanced degrees. He had made a major break through in his life and was the first of his family ever to receive a college degree. Education has been a clarion call toward a richer, more satisfying life both aesthetically and in terms of monetary reward. Now the monetary reward part is threatened although statistics still bear out the probability of greater income commensurate with a better education.

We may oversell college education, and there are many excellent jobs that do not require college training. Hopefully in an "ars gratia artis" vein, there is something to be gained from higher education in terms of life enrichment or just the challenge of being there as long as one does not take oneself too seriously.

ASSUMPTIONS

1. People inherently have a desire to learn. Humans have an innate sense of curiosity. However, this desire to learn must be focused into an established educational path. Specific courses must be mastered; often in a sequential pattern.
2. The outcome of taking specific courses does not guarantee success in life although it may lead to accomplishment in a career field.
3. Teachers go into teaching because of a desire to encourage students to learn. This does not mean they are essentially altruistic. They have their own agendas to meet, and they like to have a roof over their heads and food to ward off hunger.

4. A person who completes more education has a greater probability of economic success in our society.
5. Actual comprehending, learning and using information must share space with social adjustment and political correctness in our schools and society.

REMEDIES FOR PITHY EDUCATIONAL PROBLEMS

Before looking at some specific tasks for those who are integral parts of the education team: students, parents, teachers, administrators and staff as well as the overall community, we can look at some general situations which, being addressed with some new action insights, might ameliorate the educational scene.

The concept of compulsory attendance laws should be reappraised from an educational perspective. No doubt from the point of view of the labor force, it is good to keep young potential workers out of the labor pool. It is also good not to have idle teenagers lounging around the community emphasizing potentially bad habits. Certainly we have passed by the time when children could be forced to labor at an early age, and everyone can accept the theory that well motivated youngsters should procure all the education they can muster.

Unfortunately that is not always the way it works on the contemporary scene. Some youngsters, and let's say beyond the age of sixteen, may be learning bad habits in school and would better profit by performing simple tasks (short of brain surgery obviously). In recent years there seem to be endless jobs in the fast food industry although the influx of adults into this work force has been a developing trend. Probably the dependability that comes from a mature person recognizing one's limitations makes for a better employee.

In other words, rather than have a student languish around the campus in frustration and boredom, the door might well be opened to allow them a "sabbatical" to find themselves . This would also stop a certain amount of the disruption of the business of schools by a renegade few and perhaps make a failing grade more meaningful.

There is an important corollary involved. The door would be open for a return to high school at logical points, usually the beginning of a new semester. Some states such as California already have a proviso that a non-high school graduate may attend the junior college (and finish pre-requisite high school work) when reaching the age of 18 1/2. The concept of a CCC type program or other community service might also be offered to such youngsters to help them mature successfully.

Obviously keys to a successful school are excellent teachers, administrators and school staff members. A teacher must be competent in a subject area, but not necessarily brilliant. Being able to work with students, call this methodology, is critical at the elementary and secondary level. Motivators short of magical workers are always in demand, but we cannot expect teachers to compete with the entertainment world. A good working environment where the opinions of individuals are respected is crucial to a good school. Naturally a decent physical environment and adequate-to-excellent equipment helps. Salaries are significant but not the where all and end all.

Regrettably the teaching profession can be its own worst enemy. Teaching salaries have developed well in recent decades. A teacher will never be fabulously wealthy, but they can be comfortable. Certainly in the more enlightened states and around New York and New England salaries well up into the sixty thousand dollars range exist for the ten month school year. Educators sometimes do not like to realize that they are in the social service sector and probably will not be compensated as high as free enterprise risk takers such as doctors and lawyers (or even major league ball players). Compared with ministers, nurses and social service personnel the salaries are ok, but some remedies can be offered to improve the salary area.

In most school districts the "apprentice" program, that is the time to reach the top of the salary schedule is far too long, often twelve to fourteen years. Furthermore, the nature of teaching makes it difficult to offer greater pay for "inspired" service, and salary schedules are locked in. Obviously a husband and wife teaching team, both at the top of the salary schedule, have a different problem from a single person or an individual supporting a family. As a district superintendent, I have had a few teachers, facing bankruptcy and offered a summer job, assure me they did not become teachers to have to work even in education in the summer. (Incidentally, one man, seeking greater income, apparently found it by becoming a male madam at a brothel in Nevada).

So the task may be to find supplementary challenges for teachers who are extremely competent and want or need more income. Such opportunities may come through department chairperson responsibilities, team leaders, mentor teachers, curriculum writing, coaching, night school, summer school and correspondence programs. An alert community, seeking to enhance the school-business relationship, might also seek to find stimulating summer employment for teaching staff who would profit from a different type of assignment.

Generally what makes a better school? The answer may sound very stuffy, but I am not running for political office. The answer is better clients. Obviously schools whose parent group includes educated professionals with many two parent families will "test out" better. To assume that they have better teachers per se is rather naive, nor can the most motivated and entertaining teacher in the world overcome much of the problems associated with inner city schools. Occasionally a miracle worker comes along, and what they have should be bottled, if "it" can be identified.

Those districts which have placed a strong effort at curriculum development often are more successful. If a planned course of study is made available with plenty of options for the varied techniques of differing teachers, the results are generally better. This also assures the community that important segments of any specific course will be covered.

Schools which have fired up parent groups also fare better. There is little substitute for lay leadership to back up the teaching teams. One of the gutsiest decisions I have ever seen made came through one school district where the parents and teachers voted to turn off home televisions for a month. Believe it or not, everyone survived, books were read that had been put aside for years, and families actually communicated. Of course, this radical idea cannot work everywhere for it does take courage and self sacrifice among Rosanne watchers.

The "year around" school has also been working well in many places especially at the elementary school level. The historic American summer vacation, developed when the kids were actually needed on the farm, has really outlived its usefulness, and studies have shown that children do forget less if the gap in their programs is smaller. Other nations have proved that longer days and longer school years result in better education, but time (and money) do not necessarily beget better programs.

Beware the modern innovation. Over a number of years education has been strewn with bodies of ideas gone amok: PPBS, modern math, probably metrics, values clarification, daily demand scheduling come to mind. A dedicated zealot can make strange ideas work, but programs must be designed for overall practicality. Certainly training children to use only calculators instead of understanding that one plus one can be learned at the rote basis whether or not a machine is at hand is not in their best interests.

A word might be said about college teaching. Some higher education purists believe that if a person knows enough he or she can automatically be a good college teacher. That is rather simple. One fact has been obvious and that is that a number of college profs have a very light load. Generally speaking a high school teacher carries twenty-five classroom hours a week and a junior college teacher may teach fifteen. One would think that a college teacher could handle twelve hours, but on many campuses the load is nine, six or less. Oh yes, you will hear about all those committee meetings and research responsibilities. I had a full professor at the University of Southern California whose entire load was met by his being on campus on Wednesday. Undergraduates often do not meet their illustrious senior profs mentioned in the catalogs until grad school. If one is concerned about college costs and the quality of education, these might be addressed by courageous college boards of trustees, for it will not be faced by the American Association of University Professors.

Often the better high school students in their later years are allowed to waste their time by being teacher aides or have minimum days. Surely there must be courses by which these students can profit. Some take advanced placement courses and gain advanced college credits. Others do work at the junior college in conjunction with their upper grade high school years.

In addition to the three Rs and basic courses, schools should look at consumer economic education, health education and career education. These are not frills when the general level of information on these topics in the land is woefully low.

One can make a sure case that the schools should not have to expend any energy on moral development (the parents and churches task), but fewer and fewer students have church homes or well functioning family units. The matter is controversial, but reality is that the schools are the only entity in the land reaching almost every child. Only when entry to the school was threatened for children who did not have their basic shots was the anti-polio campaign a full success.

From time immemorial young people at age twelve or thirteen have been judged to "come of age". This was the time for confirmation in a church or bar mitzvah. So perhaps our society should recommit itself to the concept that by age twelve a young person can know right from wrong and be responsible for himself or herself in many ways. One way is to take charge of their own education. This is the key to a revitalized educational program for the United States. Without it, nothing can work. Remedies for the various component parts that make up the equation in terms of improving education follow.

THE CLIENT (STUDENTS)
1. Commit yourself to the concept that education is a high life priority—the basic job that youth have.
2. Learn to compete with yourself to constantly improve. (The top student that I ever had as a teacher, when appraised that he scored 99 out of 100 on a test and the next highest student scored 95, did not "crow" about his score, but rather wondered why he missed the one question!)
3. Commit uninterrupted, self disciplined time to your task of study. (This is the way successful artists, writers, and Olympic athletes work!)
4. Homework should not be limited to the specific tasks teachers assign, but to that range of information you are attempting to master in your varied subjects, as well as other broadening exercises such as vocabulary development, general reading, and spelling review. Your mind works best in a quiet environment..no TV or music. If the math teacher assigns you half the prob-

lems in an exercise and time allows, do them all.

5. Accept teachers as mortals with normal frailties and flaws. Give them the benefit of doubts (which may be reciprocated when you need the experience).If you are moved to attack them, do it with kindness. (The shock may be overwhelming!)

6. Consider your parents and siblings as allies.

7. Just say NO to distractions and keep your sacred appointment with yourself at your study time.

8. Fight the addiction to television and music which afflicts so many of your peers. (The top grad recently at the University of California thanked his parents for removing television from his life).

9. Seek cultural enrichment beyond your home. Stretch your wings. Don't worry about being considered a little eccentric by your peers. The people who count, especially yourself, know what is important.

10. Watch your nutrition and physical conditioning.

11. Don't be a whiner. "I am bored! That's not cool! Why don't they build me a youth center?"

12. Avoid drugs and alcohol. Not everyone is doing it, especially those who have common sense and wisdom.

13. Be alert to your growing sexuality, but do not pander to early, pointless experience or succumb to the siren song of casual sex. There will be a better time and place.

14. Consider yourself part of a family unit, share home tasks, display initiative. A critical learning variable for a successful life is learning to coexist and perhaps ultimately be a decent parent.

15. Learn to be an appreciative person—the greatest two words in the English language may be "thank you".

16. Walk in the "shoes" of your family and friends. Other people have needs and feelings.

17. Become a voracious reader and learn how to read better—faster and with more comprehension at the level needed.

18. Set your educational and life goals—near and long term.
19. Seek quality friendships with people who have positive values.
20. Never hesitate to ask for information that you need.
21. Know what is going on in the community, the state, the nation, and the world. Being an informed citizen is a requisite for a member of a free society. (One of the most amazing women I have ever known found a job as a teenager so she could subscribe to *Time* magazine. In the depression years her family was very poor. Later she worked her way through college with a job in a slaughterhouse slashing the throats of pigs. Could the words "dedication to education" apply?)
22. Become a giving person. Volunteer for community services. Coach younger children. College admission officers are also impressed by young people who help others, but the real value is within oneself.
23. Develop a musical appreciation and preferably a skill—read music, vocalize, play an instrument.
24. Analyze your interests and abilities in terms of potential career development. Making many changes in your college courses and majors is painful and expensive.
25. Understand your family's financial status and how you may contribute. College can be a very expensive experience.
26. Don't be bogged down by the academic and personal mediocrity you may see around you.
27. Develop a good vocabulary and spelling skills. The common denominator among successful people regardless of the amount of formal education is a strong vocabulary.
28. Hone your writing skills.
29. Be alert to opportunities.
30. Learn how to manage time. Use available classroom time effectively.

31. Give yourself some time to introspect and "medi-tate". Come to some accommodation with religion realizing that "man does not live on bread alone".
32. Think "selfless" and not "selfish".
33. Above all else, assume responsibility for yourself and your education!

THE PARENTS ROLE IN THE EDUCATIONAL PROCESS

1. Provide the most stable possible home environment with a structure and established routines. For example, try to have a family evening meal as often as possible at a set time with no interruptions (certainly NEVER TV). Occasionally establish a dinner topic for discussion and anticipate that everyone will have something to say.
2. Subscribe to newspapers and magazines and expect them to be utilized.
3. Perhaps a "rewards" program can be established to encourage reading. (One of my elementary school chums was given a small monetary award for each book he read. At the time I thought such "bribery" might be bad, but he emerged as our graduation vale-dictorian and an amazingly well rounded man who was voted the most likely to succeed.)
4. Minimize TV impact on the family. If it cannot be eliminated, at least control the "wasteland" to certain times and shows.
5. Establish study hours and a quiet place for your student-children to work by themselves. Do NOT buy into the "there's no homework assigned" trap, for there is always something which can be done if only reading a book.
6. Be alert to what the teachers' expectations might be, and help the children when you are able to do so. This includes attending "back to school nights" and teacher conferences.

7. Do not allow the term "boredom" in your home!
8. Make sure your students know what their parents do in the work world and learn something of their family history.
9. Remember, you are IN CHARGE. This is not negotiable.
10. Children want things to protest about. This is normal. More important, they want the feeling of parental control and firmness which is their protection.
11. Do not try to buy love. Working and single parents seem to want to compensate through "give away programs." Bright children are willing to work this.
12. Be sure your children have their assigned home tasks.
13. Assure your children that you do not like surprises. If there is a school (or any other) problem, face it head on and early.
14. Be supportive of your children, but also back their teachers and school personnel.
15. Do not speak disrespectfully of their teachers nor allow the children to do so in your presence.
16. Provide the tools of learning in as much as possible. This includes the dictionary, resource books such as atlases, perhaps an encyclopedia set, and more and more today, a computer. Some of these could be presents for Christmas, birthdays and holidays or special events.
17. Protect them from interruptions of their study schedules.
18. Have a strong expectation for reasonable school accomplishments and commend them when they do well.
19. Make sure they are aware when there are household problems since your family group is a key part in the educational team.
20. Single and working parents are no less valuable than "stay at homes", but need to be alert to the quality

of time together since there may be limitations on the quantity.

THE TEACHER'S COMMITMENT

1. The teacher should understand the team concept involving student, parent, teacher and administration.
2. Have high (but realistic) expectations of your students.
3. Realize that no one student can be allowed to bog down the group. Individual attention may have to be given on the student's time.
4. Cover the material expected in the course. Obviously all the material may be important as the building stone for the next course, or the information necessary for achievement tests.
5. Provide time for personal conferences.
6. Do not be faked out by excessive "I don't understand" demands.
7. Good achievement should be possible from not only text readers but also class listeners.
8. Do not give away grades in an attempt to be popular. Only at Lake Woebegone are all students "above average".
9. Be positive.
10. Avoid being judgmental. The child may not wind up on "death row" despite your wondering.
11. Students should know what is expected of them (and consistency is a key).
12. Every teacher should be a reading , a writing, and a current events teacher. We do not work in a vacuum.
13. Communicate with parents when there is a special need.
14. Commendation can work like that "teaspoon of sugar". Can you find something nice to say about every student every few days? Are you aware of their other activities and achievements at school and in the community?

15. Try harder for life's "underdogs".
16. Provide firm discipline and a good classroom environment.

ADMINISTRATOR MEMBERS OF THE TEAM

1. Back the teacher consistently (up and until the time the teacher must be dismissed if that ever happens).
2. Provide the space and equipment for education to take place.
3. Provide a good overall school environment and firm discipline.
4. Encourage strong parent support and leadership as individuals and through organizations.
5. Communicate the school success story to the community, but do not hide shortcomings as you work to overcome them.
6. Publicly commend your students and staff as "good things happen".
7. Expect teachers to follow the curriculum and cover the material assigned.
8. Involve the staff in decision making, hiring and planning.

THE COMMUNITY

1. Support the schools!

CHAPTER 3
CRIME AND PUNISHMENT

*A*s the twentieth century ends, a primary concern of Americans is crime in the United States. It has not been the first chapter in this Remedies treatise, however, because if we were able to remove or sharply minimize poverty, illegitimacy and illiteracy in the nation we would move toward solving most crime problems. Therefore, the Baby Licensing offered in Chapter One and improving American education in Chapter Two would move us ahead. The century has not turned and problems remain, so an analysis of crime, criminals, punishment and redemption toward remedial action is desirable.

No litany of the growing crime problem nor massive statistics will be provided. The American media delight in keeping us informed and shocked, and as in the Vietnam war, a bountiful diet of mayhem is dumped upon us on the evening news nightly. C-Span carefully presents the pontificating of the Congress on this popular topic of crime, and TV movies rapidly appear to fictionalize the sordid tales of woe seemingly moments after the print has dried on the front page. We shall look at the general problem regarding crime and then attempt to develop areas where the status quo could be improved.

Guns still seem to be the weapon of choice in the land. We do not see too many people done in by stoning or being crushed under telephone books. Knives are right up there probably because they work and are generally available, but guns work faster and more effectively. A rather antiquated provision of the Constitution written at a far different time and place referred to the right to bear arms in the context of a militia, well removed from the technology of modern warfare. Militias can be mobilized to produce an instant army in certain places in the world, notably Switzerland, but the downfall of the purportedly "evil empire" has negated the rationale that arms control is a communist plot to take over the land. Recent legislative action in terms of the Brady Bill, delayed for years by THE lobby, shows some moderate form of progress, but TV news claimed that upwards of a million AK 47s were imported and sold in the United States before the barn door was latched.

The late years of the twentieth century development of "Three Strikes and You're Out" has seemed a positive panacea until rational minds assess the potential cost of developing massive new prison colonies. An extremely controversial area is introduced with the ongoing discussion of legalizing drugs, but the area must be assessed, for most prisons are filled with drug users and sales reps, and many crimes are perpetrated to finance drug habits. Since this book is willing to assess any possible remedy, the intent will be to consider decriminalizing drugs. Is there a parallel with keeping drugs illegal and other attempts to legislate morality such as prohibition, prostitution, abortion and related issues?

The best source of new criminals seems to be jails, for the recidivism rate in our country is staggering. Rehabilitation efforts have generally been ineffective, and it is obviously difficult to impossible to find communities and employers willing to welcome felons with open arms. "Not in my neighborhood" runs rampant. Incarceration does not change poverty, ignorance, earlier abuse, dysfunctional families, and defeatist attitudes. The Horatio Alger spirit and willingness to rise from the ranks does not seem to be a common denominator in the "pen". Skills training other than how to be a better criminal has not been effective in prisons.

Criminals seem to be generated at a younger and younger age, and the inner cities apparently are covered with "wall to wall" gangs, each hell bent to out graffiti another group. The schools have been invaded, and proving manhood or membership qualifications can easily result in capital crime. Now the female element has been introduced and we all remember how much of a pain Bonnie proved to be while working closely with Clyde. Ma Barker's granddaughters may have come of age. Drive-by and freeway shootings are proliferating, and it makes one wonder whether gun licenses are being issued with driver's licenses. What happened to simple slumber parties?

Most Americans favor the death penalty for major capital crimes although not too many would be willing personally to pull the switch. We cannot decide whether or not capital punishment deters crime, but it surely must for those who cross home plate. The problem is why so relatively few cross home plate. We are so concerned with crossing Is and dotting Ts, that the prisons are filled with prisoners awaiting their umpteenth appeal. The good news has to be that huge numbers of America's burgeoning lawyer corps are provided an opportunity to put to good work the "loophole" course provided by the law school.

The rationale, key cop-out, collective guilt assuagement factor, and primary second guessing mode seems to be "abuse", physical or sexual. Apparently if the right buttons are pushed and one can claim an horrific childhood, anything goes, and juries can be worked as if with relatively short term courses in humanistic psychology. Father Flanagan's belief that "there is no such thing as a bad boy" may be over worked as the calendar pages draw down to the number 2000. America's obsession with "fair play", of itself a commendable quality, has led to a massive ambivalence in landmark cases.

John Bobbitt did not "rape" his wife, nor did she really perpetrate a crime in whacking his masculine member, for the juries "told us so". Likewise the Menendez brothers did not murder their parents although they admit to killing them, but these misunderstood lads were abused which explains the nightmare. Of course, the folks aren't around to "meet their accusers", but the lawyers know; trust them. A later trial corrected the Menendez fiasco. Anyone with a TV set still cannot see much justification for the beating of Rodney King, although a couple of cops did pay some price for their aggression, but a jury found that the boys in the 'hood were largely justified in pounding Reginald Denny. Obviously the trauma of the moment at least overcame the probability that you or I could pull that off where we live. Of course, the way out is probably a good lawyer and establishment of the fact that your old man looked hard at you in fourth grade. It will also help if "dad" is not close at hand with a point of view.

Supposedly the best justice is that which has some time proximity to the crime. Nationwide the courts seem woefully bogged down. Can we find a way out?

There may also be an increase in assaults where large numbers of people are attacked. Improved firepower obviously helps make this possible. Crimes against women; rape, assault, stalking, and kidnapping appear to be epidemic.

White collar crime is also a major national concern;

removed from physical violence, the emotional violence can be terribly destructive. Many senior citizens have seen their life savings obliterated. Now electronic filing of income taxes has opened an exciting new vista for larceny. Although anything negative happening to IRS does not choke the emotion of the average citizen, it still will cost every taxpayer in make up revenue.

So we have considered the ambivalence of the American people. As a school man, I quickly learned that though a key demand of the public was for "discipline in the schools", the concomitant corollary was upon occasion "but don't start with my kid!". We believe in speed limits but refuse to let the highway patrol have radar which might give them an unfair advantage.

ASSUMPTIONS

1. The majority of the criminal population is in jail for drug related offenses.
2. The recidivism rate remains high.
3. A disproportionate number of minorities are in prison for narcotics crimes, for being the child of single parent females of lower economic means, and having the wrong address (the inner cities).
4. Gangs are proliferating throughout the land.
5. No major nation in the world has the volume of hand guns loose among the citizenry as does the United States.
6. Though the majority of citizens favor the death penalty, the process for capital punishment is laborious indeed. According to *U.S News* of the 31 men executed in 1994, their average stay on death row was ten years. By 1996 3,122 convicts were on 36 death rows and the highest execution rate in the past twenty years (after the Supreme Court ended a four year moratorium on death sentences) took place in 1995 when 56 were executed.

7. Awareness of child and spousal abuse has been heightened.
8. Although deliquency in child support payments is still a major problem, many states have cracked down on "deadbeat" non-supporting parents.

REMEDIES OR PUNISHMENTS FOR CRIMES

Guns!

This may be a misnomer for any good Marine could tell us the difference between rifles and guns, but let's use the term in a generic sense. At this point, and judging the temperament in the land and counting votes in the face of the of the National Rifle Association (NRA), we will have weapons about us. Perhaps a personal disclaimer is in order before I am judged a total wimp. I have never owned a weapon other than a BB gun, but I did enjoy training with them in the military. Firing a rifle or a pistol on the firing range was a challenge and a pleasure. Carrying one around on the parade ground and cleaning the weapons was more work.

I have never been a hunter, probably because my father was not, and my one experience hunting squirrels as a kid was not totally satisfying, for I found myself rooting for the squirrels. I do not consider it sport when a human takes a rifle out and shoots rather defenseless animals. I would consider as a fascinating sport seeing the same hunter out there with a six inch blade taking on grizzly bears in the woods. Wow! What a contest! But that is not the way it works. Even a bow and arrow against a wild boar might represent a good go.

So taking away my non-weapon would not hurt me. However, I can see that target shooting or hunting appeals to many. Conceivably depending on one's neighborhood or whether one has valuables, a weapon for defense could come in handy although statistics on where the greater harm is done by misplaced usage of these weapons is mind boggling. I cannot see why people have problems with the registration process. Indeed, if the argument is that criminals would not register their weapons, then let that itself be a felony. (It often is.)

In fact the first Remedy for the"gun" problem is to heavily enforce the law that all former felons are prevented from owning weapons. The next solution would be to radically increase the cost for licenses to sell weapons, and that be limited to dealers with a retail address . No more selling from the back of a car or at flea markets.

The license to own the gun would also be quite expensive, say at least $100 a year, and perhaps as a much as registering a car in a major state like California should some states not have a hefty fee. We may be talking of multi-hundreds now. I would pay it and may, for the concept of buying a target pistol is still with me. In addition let's put a good sized tax on ammunition, perhaps something like that on cigarettes, for we know cigarettes are not good for one's health, and weapons are not either. Would twenty cents a round be prohibitive? That would put it in the range of a bucket of golf balls for true sportsmen.

Juvenile offenders for practically any crime should be prohibited from owning weapons for a number of years. Likewise no one should own an automatic weapon. In true free enterprise spirit, galleries or ranges might be developed for an ace rapid fire target practice in a supervised environment. I just don't believe one prefers to hunt ducks or deer with an AK 47.

Prisons.

If we are going to free up space in prisons for "third strikers plus", we must look at the drug situation (in the next section). However, some creative Remedies can be offered. Congressman Gingrich, and no doubt a host of others, have projected using some of the massive surplus of military bases for new prisons. It will make jobs in communities and provide support services. The danger in prisons may come from concentrating large numbers of "not too nice" people in a closed environment, and historically we have seen enough break outs (only a few relatively, but that qualifies as enough) plus many riots and the taking of hostages.

The basics in terms of a prison cell would be some kind of bunk, a light, a toilet and a boob tube (TV for the lesser informed). The latter would come under the term of in-house pacifier. Incidentally I have no reservation about putting tranquilizers in a prisoner's food although the ACLU might, but it seems to me we sacrifice something of our rights when we are locked up, the deprivation of freedom being foremost. I visualize a really simple cell, tiny and conceivably shared. Working up to a better room as it were would come through good behavior, an honest effort to learn a trade and/or educate oneself, and conceivably function on a prison or community oriented job (we have no limit to roadside litter). In other words, and to paraphrase a TV advertisement from a stock brokerage firm, prisoners can earn a more comfortable environment the old fashioned way; they can work for it. Trouble makers would start over—at the bottom rung.

In the overall physical plant prisoners need a dining area, some type of exercise facility for their physical bodies, and hopefully an environment for learning such as a library or trades center.

Degrees of security are commonplace now and that makes sense. Extensive counseling, work experience, and job training should be analyzed for effectiveness. This may be another service that can be purchased by the prisoners. Without strong individual effort toward self improvement as well as a good conduct record, maximum terms would be maintained.

Juveniles.

The age of reasoning in Judeo-Christian ethics was considered to be twelve or thirteen. Because we pamper youth, liberally apply Band -Aids, and allow young people to be "kept" until age eighteen, that age has been established as the age of adulthood for many purposes like voting. Experience for a number of states which endeavored to lower a drinking age to eighteen was so unsuccessful that the age was raised again to twenty-one. There are minimum ages for marriage and for enlisting in the service. The law often allows expunging records of juveniles and minimizing types of punishment, although for some categories of crimes and in some places, a juvenile may be treated as an adult. Juvenile names generally are not published in association with their crimes.

Supposedly parents are in control of their children, but there are times when this is extremely difficult to do. The best intended parent cannot always monitor the outside the home environment nor the associations their children form. Many parents have defaulted through their own problems, and the number of single parent families increases.

The simplest Remedy for troubled communities will be the curfew. No doubt it is difficult to enforce, but heavier fines for parents and the children themselves may finance larger patrol forces. The strongest penalties for juveniles (really for all of us) are those things that mean the most to us. Grounding driver's licenses would be a shock. Certainly juvenile offenders should not be allowed weapons. Community service (obliteration of graffiti as one example) would be appropriate punishment for careless young people who have not stepped beyond a prescribed pale.

Curfews raise the hackles of constitutionalists and the ACLU, but children do not have unlimited rights. None of us do. (For example, shouting "fire" in a crowded theater is not covered by freedom of speech!). In this case the ends justify the means. Preventing youngsters from being out there in the combat zone may minimize the combat zone.

Development of a CCC type program by state and federal, even local, governments may be a lesser expensive step. The boot camp concept has had some success.

I am always amazed by those who claim there is nothing for young people to do in a community. Review the limitations of small town or rural life some years ago. The schools have boundless activities especially in the area of athletics. Libraries may be found everywhere. Churches encourage young people even not affiliated with the congregation to become a part of things, and Monopoly and Scrabble and a million other games can make a home an activities parlor. Video is available in the humblest of homes, and movie rental stores are at every corner. With the investment of an empty can, "Kick the Can" may still be played under a street light. Does this sound vaguely like the dying gasp of an era gone by, or is there still hope?

Death Penalty.

There is nothing like non-controversial topics! The death penalty is on the books and favored by the majority of Americans, and yet we have made a mockery of it. "Cruel and Unusual Punishment" may well be subjecting a prisoner awaiting execution to a dozen years of false starts and foolish appeals. Yes, occasionally an error is found, but life is not always fair. Our system provides boundless safeguards. Certainly limiting the appeals process to a certain time period, say one year, and the number of appeals allowed would not be impossible. The courts are pointing in this direction.

With modern technology there must be a method for effecting capital punishment that is humane. The ultimate goal for the prisoner adjudged by his peers of a heinous crime is death.

The concern for racial quotas is one more effort to sow

dissension in the land. If more of one race are subjected to the death penalty than others, it is possible that there are valid reasons. It may have to do with socio-economics, single and/or unmarried parents, a number of societal issues, poor neighborhoods, or lack of opportunity. Nevertheless, a capital crime is a capital crime. Let's get on with it!

The Courts.

"Streamlining" is one name applied to improving the court process. It may mean running three shifts and creating more judges. It may have to do with increasing work loads for judges who are paid rather well. Incidentally, no one is forced to be a judge. Perhaps there could be para-professional judges who do not need to be lawyers. Minor offenses could be decided by smaller jury "committees". Higher court costs should be charged to those found guilty of crimes which would pay for more clerks, bailiffs, and judges. Judges who work more efficiently could be paid more.

Drugs.

Another non-controversial issue emerges. A personal disclaimer is necessary. I have never been involved with non-prescription narcotics. Consider this complaining for perhaps pot may have relaxed me somewhere along the way. The risks were and are too great. We have a major national disaster area with its own war being fought or a tempest in a teapot, depending on to whom you talk. The simple fact of the topic is that most of us do not have a pharmacological understanding of the issue, so we side with the angels and "oppose" legalization of this ravaging monster.

It may not be fair to compare "drugs" to "alcohol", although for the life of me, I am not sure why. Statistics reveal that there are far more alcoholics in the land than there are drug users. This might be a point for not legalizing drugs. Booze is addictive. Drugs may well be too, and a person can probably be addicted to aspirin and diet Pepsicola.

Americans must ask better questions. Does the casual use of marijuana invariably lead to the use of stronger drugs? Do marijuana users have problems similar to DUI (driving under the influence of alcohol)? Are we remotely winning the drug war? What is the worst thing that could happen if we decriminalize certain types of drugs? Could we "treat" heavy drug abusers through state sanctioned "centers" where gradually reducing doses would enable a drug addict to taper off?

Is there validity to the psychological theory that people want what they cannot or are not supposed to have? Are many crimes perpetrated by drug users seeking to pay the black market prices for drugs? (The answers here clearly seem to be affirmative).

Let's go for a possible Remedy which is to establish a three to five year period where certain types of drugs would be decriminalized and made available through authorized and controlled centers. Selling other than through the centers would still be a major crime. Anti-drug education would be improved, and treatment centers would continue to be available. Let's try it and see!!

Alcohol.

Now here we have another major problem, but too often refuse to look at it. Why is a person under the influence of alcohol who kills another person guilty of a lesser crime than someone who shoots another person? Well, legally the matter of pre-meditation quickly comes up. Remedies: Mandatory treatment for those who have accidents or abuse others while under the influence. Mandatory revocation of driver's licenses for those who persist in driving under the influence. We should have a high increase in taxes on alcoholic beverages to improve education for problems of alcohol abuse.

To repeat. History has shown us that making illegal something people are going to use does not work. In other words we cannot legislate morality (although we continue to do so in the case of drugs).

CHAPTER 4
THE PROBLEM OF ECONOMICS – GOVERNMENT & THE INDIVIDUAL

*W*e have long passed the era when an individual could be self-sufficient in this world. Perhaps a farmer of 200 years ago could come close. The age of specialization arrived, and even barter became of limited use. Some enterprising person developed the concept of money, and how it changed mankind!

However, centuries ago another enterprising soul or group of souls figured out that more services were needed than each member of society could provide for his family, and government was started. By the time our country was launched we had towns and cities, counties and eventually parishes, states and finally a federal government. For many years governments were small, democratic even when folks could gather at a town hall and make decisions, but then with larger numbers of citizens, representative government became necessary. Finally in America in the 1930s the conclusion was reached during the New Deal that social/economic decisions involving the well-being of the people could best be made for the citizenry by the government. Enter social security and other services. Taxes have been around forever it seems, "render unto Caesar what is Caesar's, but about the time of World War II, the IRS started playing a larger part in our lives.

Now as we look the new millennium in the eye, our federal government is in deep debt; the states and branches of local government are hurting. Many individuals are also in debt up to their hub caps, and the quality of our collective lives may be waning for the first time in decades. Horatio Alger, where are you when we need you? If ever a massive Band-Aid was needed to cover hurts, now is the moment. Perhaps it is time to look at some remedial possiblities "to bind up" the nation's and individual's economic ills.

Of course, there is a simple, time proven remedy—earn more, spend less—but that apparently would be far too radical. Mr. Micawber had it right in the time of Dickens; deficit spending will do one in.

A statistic popped on the scene recently, needed or not. A baby born in the United States has a $186,000 federal deficit attached upon delivery.

Let's look at some of the problems, obvious as they are before we have a crack at challenging them. In Pogo terms, "we have met the enemy and he is us". In effect we want more things from the government in terms of services for which we are unwilling to pay. Likewise, on the home front. We want more things than we can afford.

In terms of the federal government, many years have gone by since we have had a balanced annual budget. Such imbalance in turn has aggregated the debt the country carries into the five trillion dollar range, and even that is a veiled figure because the government apparently borrows the annual trust fund of social security revenues. Social security will soon be thrust into the red on an annual basis, accumulating larger deficits as "baby boomers" reach full modern maturity, if that is the appropriate phrase for grasping the OASI (old Age, Survivors, and Disability Insurance, or "Social Security") ring from the life cycle carousel.

OASI was established in the thirties on the demographic and actuarial fact of the moment that people would live but a few years beyond 65. Boy, did we fool them, and reaching 80 or 85 is no big thing. Now 125 years of age; that would be something, but science may be pointing us that way. Meanwhile the entire economic projection for funding social security is down the tubes. For years the federal government could just keep increasing the tax on individuals and employers by raising the tax rate and the ceiling on which the taxes are levied. Finally an adjustment has been projected down the line that the 65 retirement age would be revised upward.

Government spending during and since World WarII has skyrocketed. Of course, the cold war was expensive as was walking on the moon. Then many businesses and individuals must be subsidized. Everyone has heard of "entitlements", those guaranteed programs that may carry on forever, once given birth by government. There are beaucoups veterans to take care of and now the aging population, and we haven't even legislated a national health program to level out a playing field for medical problems. Pensions for federal legislators and their staffs border on the obscene.

Our pork barrels "runneth over", double and triple dipping is epidemic in the land, and politicians are "pandering" to the people to influence our lower instincts... the belief that there just might be " something for nothing" or the classic "free lunch" out there.

At least state governments have had to, by and large, "stay in the black". The peoples of various states in recent decades have had a field day passing "proposition 13s" as in California to control property tax increases if not roll taxes back. Meanwhile the infrastructure crumbles, and crime explodes. A 1996 report by the federal Government Accounting Office indicated that the price tag on fixing the one-third of the nation's public schools needing repair or replacement would be $112 billion. Students in large numbers (and a few politicians if the test given some Oregon statesmen is for real) do not know where Bosnia may be found let alone how much time we should have our troops spend there.

It was pointed out that the state of Iowa, with about 1percent of the national population, will need about $10 billion to repair its roads and highways. More than a few local school districts have gone broke.

This narrative could get depressing! The point as far as the problem goes is rather well known. The way out is the challenge, but fear not.

First , however, at the risk of further depression, let's look at the plight of living in America today as many Americans see it. A personal example may make the point. My early childhood was spent in the heartland of America during the depression. We were poor, but then everyone was poor, by and large. The nickel ice cream cone might have been the highest aspiration for some one with loose change.

Next came World War II which totally upset everything, but at least the depression was finally ended. The GI Bill of Rights enabled millions of GIs to go to college after the war. Money had been saved during the war by the GIs and folks at home what with women in the work force, overtime, and a limited amount of consumer goods to purchase. The pent-up demand for marriage, housing, cars, and goods and services burst forth on the land. I was too young for World War II, but managed to be in-volved with the Korean War—that's the one where the GIs came back more or less without syndromes which were to follow from Vietnam.

I was able to get an education, find a job, get married, buy a house, and have three children. My jobs changed, we aged, our houses got bigger and we kept making money as we sold the older houses. It was difficult to go far wrong. Tomorrows seemed to offer unlimited potential, and it has been a very good life.

However, my three children and now six grandchildren are not finding the going so smooth. What has happened to the American dream?

Houses are harder to reach because down payments seem harder to accumulate. The price of houses, once bought, do not eternally go up as they did in "the good old days". Many industries are being downsized, staffs cut loose, and pay scales dropped. The goods can be made in a foreign country cheaper. We all could predict that the demand for anvils, buggy whips, and corset stays would drop as technology advanced, but who would have dreamed that auto workers and steelmakers would fall on such hard times. Blue-collar twenty dollars an hour jobs have been lost. Fringe benefits have been reduced. Meanwhile daily the mail brings in a new supply of credit cards so we can borrow more at huge interest rates.

Bankruptcies have become epidemic in our land. The lotteries are taking money from the baby's milk fund, homeless for whatever reason abound, and a narcotics industry has encouraged participants to rob to get the cash to get the fix.

One must look at the number of broken homes, indifferent child support payers, and now another epidemic of children having children, notwithstanding better birth control opportunities than ever before in our history (the pill!). Retirement planning is subordinated to meeting next week's bills.

When government employees became the hostages in a congress versus the president struggle, it became quickly apparent that there was truth to the observation that most Americans are two pay checks away from the streets. That is a frightening thought.

We have reached the point where a sandwich generation has been created. Many individuals arriving at the retirement age must take care of their aged parents AND their adult children.

Let's look at some Remedies for the problem of government and individual finance. Stand by for some pain!

ASSUMPTIONS

1. Government is intended to serve the people, not be its master.
2. Government salaries and retirement plans, because of built in security, should logically trail the private sector, not far exceed it.
3. Many of our government "entitlements" have reached "sacred cow" status.
4. There are powerful lobbies at work to resist any effort to nudge their constituency groups to a modified position.
5. Retired politicians, having left office voluntarily or by popular vote, and retired military personnel have seemingly endless opportunities to double or triple dip through government jobs or jobs dependent on federal funding as in military oriented industries.
6. Individual congressmen (and women) wish to see government largesse reach their districts. This practically guarantees their reelections.
7. Conflicts of interest abound in many government entities.
8. Welfare is a big and expensive business.

REMEDIES FOR ECONOMIC WOES:
FEDERAL GOVERNMENT

1. Balance the federal budget annually. This will obviously take a bi-partisan effort.
2. Develop a very simple presentation of why all Americans must make sacrifices to implement this balanced budget. It should have the priority of announcing a war! Have this broadcast at half time on super bowl

Sunday and pre-empt time on all other channels. Ask all newspapers to present the material the following day. The point is that not only is our nation threatened now, but also the future lives of all our children and grandchildren are in jeopardy.

3. Insist that congress maintain a "by line" veto power for the president. The Republicans saw the logic of this when a Republican was president, but lapsed into forgetfulness when a Democrat was elected to the presidency. This seemingly has become a reality.

4. All federal salaries including those of the president and congress would be reduced by the percentage amount the federal expenses are out of balance on an annual basis.

5. Retirement benefits for federal employees, once the base retirement amount is established would be increased 2 percent each year not compounded regardless of the cost of living and would never exceed 75 percent of the then current salary for that position.

6. Prior to any reduction in federal taxes and after the budget is balanced annually, an amount equal to three percent of the annual budget would be applied to reduce the federal deficit.

7. Certain government services such as education would be turned back to the states and the Department of Education would be disbanded. Welfare would also become the responsibility of the states.

8. Many government services such as national parks should be privatized and pay their own way (such as the post office has done).

9. Subsidies for agriculture would be reassessed toward making agriculture self supporting. In no case would any farmer receive more than $75,000 total support in any year, and this would be for active farmers who personally work their farms. Apparently some action on this front is taking place.

10. The federal government would go on "zero based budgeting"; that is justify its budget from base zero, every year.
11. Honest royalties must be paid for mining leases on federal lands; likewise an honest land lease value for grazing cattle on federal lands would be effected.
12. No federal employee including members of the armed forces and the congress upon leaving their federal post could take a federal job or work for a company which does more than 10 percent of its business with the federal government. Likewise no retired or resigned federal employee could take a job as a lobbyist before the congress.(The assumption here is that there are plenty of qualified personnel in this nation who can fill government jobs including the job of congressman.)
13. Term limitations would be imposed on the Congress of the United States even if this requires a constitutional amendment.
14. Military procurement for the armed forces cannot be dictated by congress in excess of the professed needs established by the joint chiefs of staff. (This would curtail pork barreling with military procurement and eliminate unneeded bombers and submarines, as an example).
15. Federal government salaries would be determined by a bi-partisan board (similar to the federal reserve board) who would keep in mind competitive salaries in the private sector and the degree of security a government job provides including fringe benefits. (It might be necessary for a period of time to establish a two tier pay schedule as the new schedule is locked in.)
16. A serious federal study should be made on the decriminalization of marijuana. Since a high proportion of the residents of prisons are involved with drug

related crimes, a nonemotional based objective study should be made. (Ed. note: as mentioned, the writer has never taken illegal drugs, and abhors the drug scene in our nation).

17. OASI funds collected annually will be placed in an appropriate trust fund managed by an independent agency and made unavailable through loan to the federal government. Investment of the funds may be made in the private sector.

18. A maximum of $200 can be donated to a political campaign by an individual or a PAC.

REMEDIES FOR ECONOMIC ILLS: STATE AND LOCAL

Many of the remedies for federal government problems could also apply to the states, especially those which do not have a balanced budget requirement.

1. State departments of education would service county or multi- county levels of education. They would establish the curriculum for the state schools.

2. Under welfare:

a. A computer system coordinated with a national base and tied in to social security identification would track those who do not make their child support payments. Pay rolls could be garnisheed directly.

b. Any applicant who applies for AFDC or other welfare based on a recent childbirth, prior to receipt of aid, must be willing to have a five year birth control device placed in her arm. It would also be explained that there would be no further increase in AFDC for a subsequent child birth. (This provision would be moot if a national baby license program is developed as described in Chapter 1.)

c. Welfare recipients would be expected to perform community service. It may be necessary to provide some form of day care during hours worked or prepare home bound tasks.

d. Rather than cash payments for welfare, a debit card system would be utilized. In effect rent payments and utility payments would be deducted initially. Should a person need a new rental space, provisions would be made for advancing the first and last month's rent, cost of which would be deducted from the debit card along with rent over a twenty-four month period. Foodstamps would also be taken care of by a debit card limiting the types of foodstuffs (no alcohol or cigarets) which could be procured.

3. All state lotteries would be made illegal as soon as possible.(Lotteries represent a regressive tax on the people.)
4. Many states have already enacted term limits for office holders. All states should do so.

ECONOMIC REMEDIES: FOR THE CITIZENS
An underlying hypothesis is necessary for this section:
A. People Mean Well
B. People Can Restrain Themselves
C. People can learn to be Intelligent Consumers.
1. The educational establishment should be mandated to incorporate consumer economic education as the "4th" R, responsible spending. There should be units in elementary school social studies and a required course in high school with a minimum based competency test required for high school graduation.
2. No credit card can be issued to an individual until an employment or income base of $5,000 a year is determined for the applicant.
3. Credit card limits will be determined based on income.
4. A family may be issued only one general purpose credit card. (This would be monitored such as having one basic company for long distance phone service or one medigap carrier coordinating with medicare.). Com-

petition, of course, would come as to which company would be authorized by each family.

5. All employers would be encouraged to promote savings and retirement plans for their work force.
6. Everyone would be encouraged to tithe to himself/herself, saving if possible ten percent of his/her net income. (One major insurance company, in its advertising program, printed a statement that if such a savings rate seemed impossible, the person should "get a second job". Rather radical, what?)
7. Casino gambling would be taxed like cigarets and liquor to discourage gambling.
8. Bankruptcies would be kept on the books, so that should someone turn around their fortunes, they would be responsible for meeting old debts.
9. Those who declare bankruptcy, and those who apply for welfare should be required to attend adult "consumer economic education courses", to be paid for by the participants.
10. Dead beat child support payers would be tracked as described above.
11. Debit cards would be made available to insure that basic bills are paid by welfare recipients and others who request them (see above under local and state government).

In our nation a person who is frugal and saves his money is penalized. A spendthrift can be rewarded by welfare, free medical service, and free legal advice, while savings interest is taxed. Nevertheless, building up some type of nest egg takes care of emergencies (the major budget category, it seems), and enables one to have an enriched if not early retirement. Some people do not realize that social security was never intended to function as a full retirement plan.

CHAPTER 5
ON CONFLICTS OF INTEREST

*A*n important aspect of the human condition is Conflict of Interest. Generally we recognize this, especially when someone is clearly trying to sell us something. The less subtle conflicts may create more of a problem, identification wise.

Occasionally a surgeon might suggest some surgery, perhaps removing a gall bladder, an appendix, radical mastectomy or even a coronary bypass that might not truly be needed. As a general practitioner associate of mine once commented, surgeons really believe cutting will take care of many of our ills. Experience for the surgeon is gained and office overhead met. Likewise, a psychologist, counselor or even chiropractor needs to have an ongoing flow of repeating patients, and generally no harm can be done, other than to the patient's wallet. The tort action attorney obviously is anxious to cater to your physical and psychological ills, to the point of working for no charge (well, perhaps 40 percent as a "modest" contingency fee if he is successful in court or, more likely, defendant's insurance carrier settles out of court.)

"Caveat Emptor", let the buyer beware, may be an increasingly critical concept in the new century as more people have to hustle to survive. Buying a great acreage under that lake in Florida will continue to be a foolish challenge, and time-shares proliferate. Clunky cars still are driven by that "little old lady from Pasadena". It is to the advantage of our stock brokers for us to "churn" our portfolios, and the retail merchandise world can be loaded with booby traps. Now we can even buy hot VCRs on the corner, in many cases newly ripped off by junkies needing a fix.

I once visualized that buying something from a very prosperous individual would give me better odds at dealing with an honest person. It became apparent that those who have a fair amount find the accumulation of even more a strong challenge; in other words, there are no guarantees other than through personal diligence.

Any sales person working on a commission has the opportunity to sell an inferior product for a higher rate of commission; after all, everyone has to survive if not thrive.

Even ostensible charities may not be what they appear on the surface. The peace officer's circus may be run by a shady outfit that gives the charity pennies on the dollar for the use of their name. Comes to mind the line from the old movie when the dowager was told she would be given money for her favorite charity for her endorsement of a product. Her classic response was, "My favorite charity is me!"

Politicians are notorious for offering something for nothing which is what a distressing number of Americans seem to want to hear.

Often in male—female relations much "quid pro quo" takes place. Males have been known to proffer touching lines to curry favor, if not actually offer goods for services to be rendered. Traditionally women have thought of security if not commitment as an ulterior motive for their attitude if not behavior. More on this topic in a later chapter.

ASSUMPTIONS

1. Almost every human being is subject to a "conflict of interest" as a seller or as a buyer.
2. Hopefully a "quid pro quo" environment is possible. We receive something as we give something. Ideally we should be involved in "win-win" situations.
3. It is incumbent on the buyer to sort out degrees of conflicts of interest as the buyer spends money. We want our suppliers to realize a fair profit. That is what makes our nation function. However, we must eternally be cognizant that there are few free lunches.

REMEDIES FOR THE CONFLICT OF INTEREST ISSUE

1. A good start would be the Golden Rule: Do unto others as you would have them do unto you. Unfortunately a regrettable number of opportunists have modified this to"Do unto others before they do you".
2. Laws often have been added and/or should be added to the books to give a person an escape clause before a contract actually can be enforced. For example, in the matter of time-shares, usually a week's time is offered for a person to rethink their purchase.

There are few products being sold today with a higher pressure sales program than time-shares. This also explains why there is a vast resale market, often from buyers who should not have taken the plunge, whereby you can procure time share units for pennies on the dollar. People succumb to the siren song, and sink in way over their heads. Sales people, with "high sales quotas or lose your job", gloss over the fact that the $10,000 unit purchased often carries a $500 annual maintenance and tax fee, another fee to join an exchange club, a fee to make the exchange if that is the goal. Even the use of your $10,000 cash purchase price is worth $500 to $600 a year in interest lost. The math is even rougher if one buys a time share on "time". There usually is a poor resale market and it may cost a ton to get to the location (as my friend who bought an inexpensive time-share in South Africa is finding out).

3. Any medical opinion that necessitates surgery or extensive repeat visits would benefit from second and third opinions.
4. The English system should be introduced so that anyone initiating a spurious lawsuit who loses would pay the defendant's cost. Lawyers on a contingency fee would have to pay half the cost (see the later chapter on the "law").

Many American lawyers, especially those whose specialty is chasing ambulances, insist that any poor man should have the right to sue. The poor man's right supposedly would be lost if he were responsible for paying a defendant if he as plaintiff lost the case. If the case had merit, then anyone should be willing to take the risk if one felt aggrieved. And who covers the poor man being sued who must pay a large legal fee, preponderately to an attorney, even when winning? Unfortunately lawyers become legislators and judges, and as legislators receive huge contributions from trial lawyers. This may be the ultimate in "conflicts of interest".

5. Commission structures should be listed in the boiler plate in a sales contract.
6. Known defects should appear in a disclaimer for various products. More and more often this is required in real estate contracts.
7. "Worst case scenarios" should be described and are generally mandated for prospectuses on various investment products.
8. No-fault insurance is an idea whose time has come. One can make a case that a spurious or fraudulent claim should always be fought, but in the no-fault environment, attorneys are neutralized. Needless to

say, trial lawyers are the major obstacle to passing no-fault insurance laws.

9. Never should a monetary award exceed the amount necessary to offer an injured claimant a decent life style. Outrageous awards in court have placed a huge price tag on many goods and services, and in some cases have even eliminated vital services because of the potential for ridiculous awards. We might refer to this as the McDonald's hot coffee syndrome.

10. Approach "love" cautiously. Pre-marital agreements should be utilized for any permanent entanglements. (This probably is a man's viewpoint, and I am told that if one truly "trusted" the other it would not be necessary. In my view if you truly trust the other person, you can safely summarize your points of agreement. It can eliminate "games" on both sides.)

CHAPTER 6
MEDICINE

I must confess a bias. Of all the professions, the one which I hold in highest esteem is medicine. In part this is because I have known and been treated by such dedicated, competent, and caring people over the years. In part it is because I stand in awe of not only their training, just short of forever and ongoing beyond that, but also because of their tireless hours—early in the day to look in on patients in the hospital, then to the office, perhaps some surgery, then back to the patients and calls beyond that. Finally I could never be a medical doctor because I do not have that confidence in myself that I want in my doctor,—and digging into the body with ensuing bloody exposure is not my cup of tea. In fact, dissecting frogs and cats escaped me in high school.

I want my doctors to be very well reimbursed—well, perhaps not quite as well paid as someone really important like the center fielder for some major league baseball team.

Modern medicine has moved light years ahead in this century, and yet there are major challenges unmet. We have trouble handling the common cold and lower back problems. Creative inroads have been made in the fight against cancer and heart disease and yet new nightmares such as AIDS creep into our vocabulary. What we have done is move our life span to an age unimaginable at the turn of the century. Miracle drugs help offset even our most marked foolishness. The disease of overeating, often a head trip, will be countered by new pharmaceutical ventures. Unfortunately attacking other human aberrations such as addiction to smoking, alcohol and narcotics may have lost ground.

Now new moral dilemmas are being thrust upon us. The very act of dying is a puzzlement, and at what point can we just let go? Living wills are being suggested so that people might be allowed to die before total disability, physical and/or mental, takes place. When should heroic measures be taken to prolong an almost non-life? Economics must enter the equation, for vast sums of money are being spent in the final chapters of our lives. How much can the public afford? Former Governor Lamm of Colorado spoke forthrightly of ultimate limitations in care, and yet some perceived him as heartless. The state of Oregon has made an effort to catalog and prioritize and limit medical procedures, beyond which the state cannot afford to offer its citizenry.

Assisting the final stages of death is a raging controversy. When does assistance become euthanasia?

Health care is very expensive and arguments over the funding of medicare have fueled great partisan debate to the point of threatening the operation of the government. Yet, everyone agrees that medicare is on a collision course with economic collapse. The spectre of eroding medicare is held up as a vast bogeyman to seniors. We are unable to decide on a federal health plan. A few unscrupulous health care givers have milked fortunes from the existing system. Long term care is another significant controversy as to who pays.

We are wising up, at least at one level, to proper nutrition and diet. Fat is Mr. Ugly, and yet the masses persist in frequenting Mr. Fat's favorite stamping grounds, the fast food parlours of America. More fat farms are being organized for young children whose sedentary preoccupation with television and nintendo threatens their well being.

Finally, we have reached the point with the computer where interlinkage enables medical researchers to know almost immediately what progress others are making in specific fields. The wheel need not constantly be reinvented at many different research sites. Breakthroughs should come sooner, more efficiently and effectively.

We look anew at holistic medicine and realize that the wisdom of the ages has some merit. Alternative medicine has a potential in many fields.

There may be too many hospitals competing for patients whose stays in the hospital are being shortened, if not eliminated by outpatient surgery and clinics. Modern hospital equipment is extremely costly, and a minimum number of beds for efficiency should be a reality. Still proprietary interests and loyalties keep marginal facilities functioning. New ventures such as health maintenance organizations are either praised or damned.

The sticky wicket of unnecessary litigation is a nightmare hanging over medical practitioners and institutions. The chapter on the law will assess this concern.

The subject of dentistry will be touched obliquely. I recently visited an oral surgeon who told me that when he began his practice twenty years ago, if a child came into his office with perfect teeth, the dentist would gather the entire staff to observe. Now because of fluoridation and improved care almost all children have good teeth. Many dentists are becoming specialists—oral surgeons, periodontists, endodontists, and orthodontists. It is a major successs story. Full dental plates may become a dying art form. Huzzah!

ASSUMPTIONS

1. Computer aided research will advance breakthroughs in critical areas.
2. Consensus can develop priorities for health care. We may not be able to afford every procedure for all ages. Life is a journey; we know the destination, and when our time comes we just get on with it.
3. There necessarily is a point of diminishing returns in offering health care.
4. There are limits as to what we can do.
5. Each person should be responsible for his/her own health.
6. Extended families can and should help take care of each other.

REMEDIES FOR MEDICINE AND HEALTH PROBLEMS

1. Our schools must do an infinitely better job in teaching health education (along with the 3Rs, consumer economic ed and career ed). To see young children start smoking or drinking or get into drugs is a tragedy. Yes, parents should be involved, but the schools have access to almost every child, and we are blowing it.
2. The United States must develop a national health program to equalize our opportunities (this from a fairly conservative writer). It must stop being a political football fueled by insurance companies and lawyers.
3. Everyone should pay something for medical assistance; some form of co-payment, to eliminate those who wish only to have their hands held.
4. Cigarets should be treated as a prescription drug. None should be made available to minors, and young people smoking should be cited and fined (as in violating curfews). Incidentally a grass roots plan to "Just Say No to Smoking" might enable young people to put a positive spin on peer pressure.

5. The citizenry should be educated further through the media such as pamphlets and television shows on good nutrition. Apparently three-fourths of adult Americans are overweight to some degree.
    a. Labeling on foodstuffs should be expanded.
    b. Bigger warnings, perhaps from the surgeon general, should be placed on Mr. Fat's fast foods.
6. Hospital accreditation should be tightened up to phase out sub-standard hospitals. Mergers should be encouraged.
7. Research coordination should be expanded and rewarded.
8. Organ donations should be encouraged; perhaps even subsidized by tax inducements.
9. Spurious litigation should be minimized by incorporating English law and placing limits on outlandish awards
10. Living wills should be encouraged (as many states do!)
11. Excessive surgery should be analyzed and limited. Special areas to be reviewed could be gall bladders, hysterectomies, prostate surgery, tonsillectomies, appendectomies, radical mastectomies, angioplasties and open heart surgeries.Okay, I am over my head, but the point is made. Let medical review boards take over—but follow up the point.

CHAPTER 7
THE LAW AND LAWYERS

*M*y feelings about lawyers are very ambivalent. Just as I believe too many today are parasites determined to cause mischief usually in their own behalf, then I find some competent and dedicated attorney. I probably have a love-hate relationship with the law as I do with journalism, and at some perverse level would enjoy being a lawyer or journalist. That may stem from an innate desire to throw things into fans to see what turns up.

There has been a proliferation of lawyers in recent years, and in their recompense a statistician can really mark the difference between the mean and the median. The average attorney is probably doing quite well because a few are doing extremely well. However, many struggle to survive; hence, the push for opening up advertising venues. Even television is engulfed with their commercials. "Neighbor look at you harshly? Let's sue the bugger!" Ambulance chasers abound in the modern age, and any hope of developing a "no-fault" insurance system which could effectively handle problems is obliterated by an onslaught from trial lawyer's groups.

Businesses have been driven into bankruptcy, worthwhile products withheld from the marketplace, competent medical practitioners have left their trade because of tort action possibility or actual experience. Outrageous and egregious awards have been given by juries which would make Robin Hood blush. Insurance fraud is rampant in the land because of the high cost of litigation.

The concept of contingency fees whereby a lawyer would not charge plaintiff for a case unless compensation is awarded at which point he or she would receive up to forty per cent of the proceeds is troublesome. Many insurance companies will settle even the most ridiculous or spurious suit since it may cost less than extended litigation, and the deep pocket will prove a continuing target. The simple answer, referred to earlier, is to switch our system to the English system whereby the defendant, in winning a nuisance suit, can claim reimbursement for attorney fees and costs. Trial lawyers do not approve of this possibility under the guise that a poor man may not be willing to take the risk, but if a suit is eminently valid, then why not?

A certain number of suits, often class actions, are intended to bring about social change through the courts. When I was a superintendent of a school district which had some semblance of a dress code, we were sued by a Native American lad courtesy of his free lawyers, the California Rural Assistance League, who established that our expectation of what we thought was reasonably long hair, was a violation of his tribal mores. Obviously it was easier to function without a dress code, but there are points of principle that should transcend ease. In this case the rationale was that it is what is in a student's head rather than what is on his head that is important. My own view, then and now, is that what is on his head also represents what is in his head. For example, green hair carries a message.

There now are so many cases before the courts that

justice represents a massive endurance contest. Apparently foremost on the dockets are drug related cases.

Surely you perceive the drift!

ASSUMPTIONS ABOUT LAWYERS AND THE LAW

1. People should have the right to legal representation and the right to have their grievances redressed by law. They do not necessarily have the right to file capricious or spurious suits as are many prisoners in jails the nation over.
2. A person filing a suit should be responsible for his action. Now it is almost impossible to countersue even against a spurious suit unless "malice" can be established and that appears to be very difficult.
3. Many aspects of law can be handled without lawyers—divorce, probate avoidance, powers of attorney, and wills to name a few. Simplification in process might add many other topics.
4. Defendants are theoretically given the right to fairly timely trials. The reality is often different.

REMEDIES FOR PROBLEMS
INVOLVING LAWYERS AND THE LAW

1. The English system should be established in the United States whereby the plaintiff and contingency oriented attorneys would no longer have a clear advantage. Compensation would be awarded victorious defendants, part of which should be paid for by the lawyers who encouraged the suits.
2. No-fault insurance laws should be implemented.
3. In seeming conflict with #2 above, insurance companies should fight fraudulent claims even if it costs more money. (Somewhere in my background I remember the sterling admonition, "When principle is involved, be deaf to expediency!")
4. Individuals filing fraudulent claims would be penalized to the full extent of the law.

5. Juries would not be required to reach a unanimous verdict in many types of criminal or civil case. (A two/thirds vote should suffice).

6. More cases should be heard by a three judge tribunal to accelerate justice and probably reach better decisions.

7. When backlogs occur in court rooms, part-time judges, retired judges, and temporary panels of judges might be asked to function. Courtrooms should operate around the clock with legal teams.

8. Bar associations should take more aggressive action against attorneys who discredit their profession.

9. Legal associations should not be allowed to make political contributions to positions (such as initiatives) in which they have a direct conflict of interest. Individual attorneys, of course, would have the right to contribute as they see fit.

10. More lawyers should be sued for malpractice, malfeasance, dereliction of duty when it appears feasible. Most of us are afraid of lawyers for they are trained to function in court. However, some effort to develop a national sue a lawyer month, of course for those with valid grounds, might underline the importance of the English system of law, and enable lawyers to share the feeling that one suit can ruin a financial future (and an otherwise good day).

CHAPTER 8
THE MEDIA AND ENTERTAINMENT

*I*n recent years there has been growing distrust of the media. Reporting news has given way to managing news, and competition among networks is strong. The newspaper industry has fallen on hard times, and many two or more newspaper cities have lost one or more of the papers reducing the level of competition. It is becoming more difficult to ascertain whether we are reading or listening to a news report or an opinion on the news. What America needs, according to the press, are more men biting dogs.

There seems to be a lessening of the educational background of the reporters; certainly this is true on television where a pretty face and charisma is more important than an education or special training. Who needs a background in meteorology when a clown suit will do? Nine second sound bytes may be all the time the busy consumer can spare for a critical issue.

Now there is also a proliferation of cable channels with more and more specialization taking place. Such competition has bred a new generation of cable hoppers. He who controls the remote control unit, controls the kingdom. It also may represent new grounds for divorce.

Talk shows have sunk to the bottom of the pit, and green haired Venusians who cross dress are the rage. Home shopping is easier than ever, and advertising minutes per hour watched on commercial television seem to spiral upward. The government is rattling the sabre at public broadcasting which in turn is looking more and more like a commercial station with special fund raising hours giving way to days, weeks and soon perhaps millennia.

Major book publishing companies continue to merge and small publishing companies emerge with self publishing reaching a new high. Short novels have captured the "go-go" time limited general environment, and Robert James Waller's *Bridges of Madison County* found more than ten million copies in print and three years on the best seller list. The silver screen continues to crank out epics and not so epics, and the home VCR movie business booms.

Magazines have had a rebirth of circulation and many special interest publications have been launched. Whether this is a genuine reaction for self improvement or a response to the proliferation of lottery-like magazine promotional contests remains to be seen.

Then we have music. My own gloomy outlook is that "rock and roll" and Newton Minow's "vast wasteland" of television may result in the decline and fall of America. As mentioned, young people who cannot possibly be expected to retain the knowledge that Washington, DC (our 51st state?) is the capital of the United States, can hear a three minute rap song once and have the lyrics down cold. "Ah, sweet mystery of life!"

Thoughts of MTV and current lyrics from the unwashed musical groups which seem to abound bring up the age old concern for censorship. What is porn? Why presume that a few million scurrilous words will hurt us in movies or in contemporary literature? One reviewer pointed out that the 1995 movie *Pulp Fiction* used the F— word three hundred times—well, perhaps it was only 298, but it was enough to worry whether the writer of the rather insipid movie thought he had a new word which might shock someone as against bore them to death.

The working press have had a liberal bias, by and large, over the years, in many instances indicating they would prefer a job with the Nottingham Gazette so they could join Robin Hood's merry men. Likewise management traditionally has loped along in tune with conservatives and robber barons. There has always been a certain amount of overlapping. The boss group is able to dictate endorsements often times, while the journeymen reporters just load their bias into what otherwise would pass as news reporting.

So the working press have managed to gain a popularity with the American people right up there with politicians and lawyers.

ASSUMPTIONS:
1. Americans are still captivated by celebrity entertainers including many reps from the fourth estate.
2. We really want to believe these good folks, and treat them like royalty.
3. There is an information overload of amazing proportions continually building through modern technology. The information highway spilleth over—watch out for more wrecks!
4. The good book has told us (John 8:32) "Know ye the truth and the truth will make you free", but where do we find the truth through media as the new century begins?

REMEDIES FOR PROBLEMS EMINATING FROM THE MEDIA AND ENTERTAINMENT WORLD
1. Purveyors of films and writers of books that use scurrilous language more than six times per book or movie should be placed in a padded cell and forced

to listen to a recording of the F— word uninterruptedly for three hours. If it is apparent they are still enjoying the experience, their mouths should be washed out with strong soap.

2. The entertainment industry including publishing should develop a new code letter which would be placed at the start of the movie (book, record) indicating that the viewer (reader, listener) should stretch their imagination and visualize all kinds of naughty talk at appropriate times so we will no longer have to be bombarded with the actual expletives.

3. Weather persons should be licensed as meteorologists or else clearly branded as song and dance persons.

4. Likewise newscasters should be required to have a license proving they have a college degree (or at least successfully matriculated from grammar school). This in turn might eliminate a few with third grade educations (along with a few Oregon politicians) who cannot find Bosnia on a map.

5. Major advertisers should band together to buy time so that periodically an hour would take place on all radio and television stations simultaneously whereby there would be absolutely no sound or pictures broadcast. However, there is a danger that minds might open up and conversation between humans and families take place.

6. More school districts should follow the lead of a few where teachers and parents have joined together to declare TV free nights (or even days or weeks).

7. Citizens should write sponsors of mindless talk shows and threaten to boycott their products. Then, if necessary, carry out their pronouncements. This occasionally has actually been done.

8. Individual Americans should commit themselves to periodic moments of media free meditation.

CHAPTER 9
ARMED FORCES & THE NATION'S DEFENSE

*W*ith the possible exception of the Spanish American War in 1898, our nation has had to be led into wars "kicking and screaming". Once the basic configuration of the 48 states was established, the Pacific Islands (Hawaii among others) absorbed, and Alaska purchased, we really had no great incentive to broaden our borders. Nature had insulated us from Europe and Asia, and separation and distance were our major allies. We have had strong cultural ties to Europe, particularly Great Britain after declaring independence from the mother country. Coming to her aid in two major wars in the twentieth century was rather difficult to arrange. Furthermore, the concept of some sort of a league or union of world nations was thoroughly repudiated by the American congress after World War I. This independent act indirectly led to Hitler's taking control of Nazi Germany and World War II.

The development of international communism consumed most of the century although it competed directly with the west only after the second world war. The United States believed that the Soviet Union was a major threat to world peace although geography per se shows that the

USSR had more to worry about than the west in terms of offensive and defensive positions. The major second world war antagonists seemed perfectly willing to use their defeated status to become nonmilitary powers, but, instead, Japan and Germany became industrial power houses. The United States bore the brunt of the world anti-communist effort. The Soviets, having run an effective race in developing their military establishment, eventually lost the economic struggle and imploded.

So what are the prospects for peace in the world, and what should America's role be in the peace process? This is probably one of the most important single political and economic questions this book addresses considering there is such an immense cost involved in fighting wars, maintaining a position whereby we could fight a war, and avoiding wars. The price tag threatens the economic future of the nation.

Fortunately an organization emerged the disintegration of world communism which can offer some prospects for peace, with a few caveats—the United Nations. Much internal house cleaning needs be done apparently, and the work force at the UN has become bloated far beyond need. The good news is that its headquarters in New York enables us to have a closer vision of how it operates. The UN was there for us when the Korean War errupted (fortunately the USSR had walked out of the security council at a poor strategic time for them). The UN has been serving as a peace keeping force in the post World War II era with general success. A major problem within the UN may come from the imbalance of third world nations for whom the scintillating story of Robin Hood holds a spell—and guess who represents the wicked sheriff of Nottingham in their eyes.

The major nations of the world have no energizing aggressive needs as the 21st century commences. England and France wrestle with internal financial problems and the common European market. Germany is undergoing a massively expensive reintegration of its Eastern sector. Japan enjoys its affluence and works to keep moving forward. China is the still sleeping giant, maintaining its communist-socialist status while becoming a major entrepreneurial force in the world. The United States is trying to balance its debt and generate a forward thrust to its economy; hardly a would be aggressor nation in the world community.

Strangely the major world problem is religion, particularly Islam in the Middle East. Poverty and a nationalistic spirit also create grievous difficulties, not only for African nations as the world has witnessed, but also in other areas like the Philippines. Population growth still burgeons in the third world although an awareness of the nagging problem is becoming a reality. Progress is currently defined as holding African families to six plus children, while many Americans display their wrath when China has made one child per family a goal (with its concomitant nightmares of human rights violations).

There are glows of progress in encouraging the Middle Eastern Arab nations to finally accept their neighbor Israel as a reality just as Israel is giving some concessions to her neighbors. However, the election of a new militantly conservative president in Israel may negate an offer to buy security by returning conquered soil

Oil is still the primary raw material in the modern world. It has created much wealth for many in the Arab block nations. This has enabled their rulers to stock pile the latest technological warfare toys including nuclear and biological weapons and potentially their source of delivery to targets anywhere in the world. Although quantities may never reach a proportion of those assembled by the US and USSR toward the end of the cold war, some tragic scenarios can still be drawn. Does anybody want to buy a surplus nuclear powered submarine capable of launching nuclear warheads? Watch the Home Shopping Network for late details.

And hatred of neighbors still runs deep in many sections of the world from African tribes, the Kurds and the Turkish (and Iraqui), and the former Yugoslav nations to display but the tip of the icebergs.

So the United States looks to its military as the armed forces face a totally different scenario from any ever presented before. After both major wars we dismantled the military to the point where we were woefully unprepared for the Act IIs. Big dollars have been involved, and it seems to be an easy target for cuts, at least for a while, and until an emergency threatens. Where bases will be maintained and what major military weapons will be constructed where, often bypasses logistics and enters the world of the political. If our new 21st century America is going to dictate "make work" jobs to keep large numbers employed, where will they be and who will decide? For years I wondered why there were still humans manning automatic elevators in the capitol building. The answer simply is that it makes jobs, and not one that requires a brain surgeon.

We must also look at what formerly was called the space race. One clear military application in theory is a star wars defense system that would protect us from errant missiles fired by some emotional third world dictator. The Patriot missiles apparently helped in the defense of Saudi Arabia and Israel against Scud missiles during the Gulf War, although there are those who doubt the total efficiency of the Patriots.

Is there a single American who is not proud that we responded to John Kennedy's challenge to walk on the moon? But where do we go for an encore and to what end? Mars? We hear of modern technology products being offshoots of the space race. At what cost velcro?

ASSUMPTIONS

1. Americans and by far the majority of world citizens want ongoing peace.
2. We do not want peace at any price—for example, at the cost of the loss of our freedom and subsequent enslavement.
3. We anticipate that we can analyze what military challenges we may face and solve them with a lean, mean efficient machine of men and materials. The Gulf War affirmed such a capability.
4. We know we must function in a world of nations. Conversely, most of us realize that we must not sacrifice our autonomy to a "one world" government.
5. We must weigh the need to reduce our debt, balance the federal budget, and yet preserve what military forces we must maintain.
6. The United States will accept its role as world super power without pushing others around. We will reason with nations as we encourage them to solve problems of overpopulation and "human rights violations". Above all else we shall endeavor to put our own house in order.
7. There are certain functions of the armed forces that can provide appropriate civilian applications (such as the Corps of Engineers of the U.S. Army).

REMEDIES TO PROBLEMS OF THE MILITARY ESTABLISHMENT

1. We would maximize an investment in "research and development" to provide twenty-first century weaponry. Likewise personnel would be trained for a different type action.
2. America should initiate a system of two year Universal training and service for all of our youth. Options for this training would be the armed forces, civilian conservation corps, religious missionary work, the

peace corps, police reserve training, and a medical emergency training and volunteer corp.

3. A massive reserve system, preponderantly inactive, would enable the nation to preserve a large, organized potential force.

4. Our armed forces would emphasize a sizeable, mobile, rapid response force with multiple options capability. It would be a volunteer force of dedicated professionals, probably based on the United States Marine Corps, Army Ranger program, and US Navy SEALS.

5. The armed forces have led the nation in equal opportunity for minorities and women. This would continue to be the case.

6. The military would establish weapons stockpile locations around the world with minimum staffs and no dependents. In fact dependents would stay at home, and service personnel in reduced numbers would have short duty periods at these locations. (By dependents staying at home, a potential conflict of interests would be avoided, acts of terrorism minimized, and a more stable life for military families would result).

7. The armed forces would concentrate on logistics. Every civilian cargo ship and commercial aircraft would be part of the reserve fleet to move forces and supplies far and fast.

8. Occupational overlapping would be broadened as in the case of the Corps of Engineers where projects with civilian application are undertaken. This could include areas of agriculture, controlling penal populations, providing community emergency services, flight controllers, providing educational aids, recreational program advisement, counseling programs, working on highways and infrastructure, and others.

9. The professional military service career could be lengthened to correlate more closely with the civil-

ian world. Higher pay would come with more time in the service. The minimum age for early retirement might be increased from 20 to 25 years, and full retirement granted at 35 years of service or age 60. Retired personnel would not be eligible for employment with the federal government or businesses having preponderantly military contracts. (The hypothesis is that there are plenty of competent personnel eligible for employment in our society).

10. Surplus or reserve military bases would be given a high priority for temporary or long term prisons or civilian training camps.

11. A GI Bill program would continue to be offered after military service.

12. The United States will aggressively seek options to minimize the use of oil by the year 2025. Research and Development will concentrate on this goal. Storage of nuclear waste will be resolved in a fail safe environment, and fail-safe nuclear energy will be expanded in the nation and in the armed forces.(The reduction in the use of hydrocarbon fuels will save lives and protect the environment!)

13. The United States will reassess its goals for space missions and minimize future space operations until it clearly can be established that a high national priority is identified.

14. All business and industry will coordinate with the Department of Defense in developing a master plan for the conversion of a civilian economy to a military one in the event of a massive world crisis (currently not visualized).

CHAPTER 10
RELIGION & MORALITY

*I*t is a sad commentary that so much grief in the world is caused by religious fervor. Most religions have basic laws that are similar. Judeo-Christian ethics would be recognized generally as logical rules under which to live, even by those who profess themselves to be non-religious. Problems arise when religions capture the state mechanism. The person or persons who interpret the religious and civil law have immense potential power.

Although the emerging United States was founded by people of different religions, basically Christian and preponderantly protestant, there was a marked separation of church and state which undoubtedly has made this nation strong. There has been plenty of room for immigrants of other religious beliefs to find a home. The United States has had no state religion. Now suddenly a crying issue before the land is whether prayer shall be legalized or even mandated in the public schools. Extreme religionists offer growing litmus tests as to whether candidates might be conservative enough, Christian enough, and even born again. This is a very dangerous trend for a country that basically prides itself on religious freedom.

Inquisitions are certainly not needed in the United States as the new millennium arrives.

An equal and opposite danger emerges when moral codes break down, when a shoddy interpretation of "values clarification" says one may make their own rules of behavior and language use, where such a a fear of censorship exists that anyone is encouraged to read and write and photograph anything, anytime, anyplace.

Perhaps the most controversial issue before the land is abortion. Undoubtedly everyone can agree on the basic tenet that one should not kill a living human being (death penalty for certain crimes excepted). However, the argument rages over whether a fetus is a human being. It has been discussed earlier that it is such a sad and unnecessary issue in that science has already provided us the wherewithall to prevent conception. It presumes a woman, and the onus regrettably is on women, who anticipates being sexually active, can count to twenty and place herself on a birth control system. In fact with the newer long term birth control implants, one does not even have to count, and "morning after"pills are now available.

Debate continues in terms of Genesis versus evolution. I believe if one can bypass the definition of one of God's work days as a technical 24 hour period and accept a longer span of time, the theories can be reconciled readily. A recent discussion with an acquaintance assured me that a day meant exactly 24 hours and the "good book" made it specifically clear. My interpretation of the bible in addition to its being a literary masterpiece, a top best seller of all books ever published, and a moderately accurate history of a period in the development of the Western World, is that it was written by men who had human frailties, and not by God Himself working on a tight production schedule.

If you manage to interpret what I have said regarding

religions, you might gather I am a protestant Christian. Just as I do not apologize for my beliefs, I do not attempt to foist them on anyone else. I do believe that it is important for a person to have some beliefs, some faith, some underlying ethic, even as we all study the great mystery of the universe. I cannot see how anyone can deny the existence of a God, a creator, a universal force, if I am allowed to define that God. In effect God is the final answer to a million questions asked by infants and senior scholars alike which start with the three simple letters W and H and Y. There are too many things happening that defy a humanly based answer starting with nature.God is the"why" beyond all things, the natural force of the universe; however, He may bear a dozen names.

Just as William Shakespeare managed to make a thousand logical judgments on the human condition in his plays, so does the bible or other guiding books of world religions offer thoughts on how to live. In addition to the basic commandments, let's look at just three. "Judge not lest ye be judged", "Know Ye the truth and the truth will make you free", and "Love thy neighbor as thyself". These might represent the most significant remedies for broad based problems imaginable.

ASSUMPTIONS
1. The human has a natural tendency to question why we are here and what is our purpose in life.
2. By far most people could meet in a large committee and develop logical laws for a society. They would be quite similar to what we have now.
3. Religion is very personal, and each human must come to some understanding of whether or not they wish to find some religious "home".
4. We must respect others in matters of customs and religions. Every old boy and girl scout knows that.

5. Likewise our lives are fuller if we not only can tolerate but also understand the richness of varied religions and ethnic traditions.
6. All humans will benefit from periods of meditation or introspection. For some this is called prayer.
7. We can never have total freedom. In other words our right to free speech does not allow us to cry "fire" without cause in a crowded theater.
8. We must live in a society of laws.It is necessary to abide by the law and respect the law even as we work to change a law with which we might disagree. Some laws relate to morality.

REMEDIES FOR PROBLEMS
OF RELIGION AND MORALITY

1. Churches and their concomitant religions must be bastions of tolerance, peace and goodwill in our communities.
2. The separation of church and state shall be maintained; however, national and ethnic holidays can be honored and traditions shared.
3. There will be no mandatory prayer in public schools. However, there should be numerous opportunities for students to meditate at a quiet time in a quiet place.
4. Public schools have reponsibility to present a broad cultural picture of our society showing the richness of its religions and traditions. Respect for the viewpoints of others must be engendered.

CHAPTER 11
MALE/FEMALE RELATIONSHIPS AND THE AMERICAN FAMILY

Among the more serious of America's ills is the decline and fall of the American family. The greater cause may simply be categorized as modern living which in turn encompasses a variety of problems. The extended family of rural times in America is gone with the wind. Marriages are collapsing at a very high rate; marriages not technically rent asunder by divorce, in too many families are not joyous relationships. Children are having children, perhaps 25 to 30 percent of whom are not married to the fathers. These facts are such common knowledge as to no longer jar the nation's collective conscience.

The problem is compounded by predictable and growing statistics that children born into poverty in single parent homes often in inner cities are mini-time bombs ready to explode. The detonation will beget further poverty, drugs, crime, more children and eventually further fan the clash between "haves" and "have nots" in our society. Now pressure is growing to reduce welfare benefits and force welfare recipients to work which exacerbates the issue.

Some radical remedies are urgently needed, but the siren song of political correctness must be played out. First, those of us ready to "fix" things must identify basic concerns as follows:

There are too many irresponsible marriages; in other words, it is just too easy to get married. Concomitantly, it is too simple to break up a marriage. It is not difficult to have children whether or not married; in fact you are rather well subsidized if you do have a child under poverty guidelines.

The good news is that women have come of age as a force in society and no longer plan to be subordinate to their male counterparts. They can procure employment in almost every field and their wage levels are rapidly catching up to those of men. They do not have to become dependent on a man for their livelihood so that bond for marriage has been passed by. As a matter of fact, they do not even have to get married, let alone stay married.

For many the concept of trying to work out problems within a marriage takes too much energy when the option out is easy.

Likewise the minimal advance planning necessary for a girl who desires to become sexually active should not be a problem. Birth control measures are readily available and practically fail safe (at least for the pill). One mother of teenaged daughters of my acquaintance told the girls that when they were teenagers and were contemplating an involvement, she would go with them to procure birth control prescriptions. According to a high school counselor friend there remains a ridiculous psychological barrier to getting birth control protection. A girl feels if she plans in advance, she is immoral; if she goes ahead spontaneously and has sex with her boy friend and becomes pregnant, that's all right. That may be a variation of the "but it will never happen to me" theme.

It is amazing that so many marriages do work out. The male-female relationship is difficult to fathom. First, of course, it is hard for the human to truly know himself or herself. Then relating to another person of the same sex is tough, but trying to figure out the opposite sex is truly difficult. Who can help out a young person? Parents can and should, but we have already given away the fact that many marriages are shattered by divorce or unhappiness, and that in too many cases there is no father figure anyway. That means the schools, the common denominator in our society, must pick up the task. Educators envy new assignments like the plague, but improved family life education courses encompassed in a sex education and health education program "must happen" in all of our schools.

Value differences must be analyzed in such a course. Men and women have differing modes of communication not even considering a myriad of personality types. Man is a predatory animal and woman traditionally is more nest oriented. A sociologist at the University of Hawaii expressed it well. "For men, sex is like basketball; it is just something to do. For women it is more of a commitment".

This projected family living-sex education course would really cover the heavy duty responsibility of having children. When I was teaching government years ago in the summer session at San Bernardino, California, High School, I was able to take the class to visit the superior courts downtown. One judge wanted to spend a few minutes with the class and explain to them the law about marriage for juveniles. Beneath a certain age, parents must give their consent to the union. Below that age the judge must agree to a marriage between younger teens. The judge stated, "And frankly I just plain turn down the request!" Responding to the predictable "why" from the students, he added, "Almost always when I sanctioned such a marriage, in a couple of years they would be back before me seeking a divorce. I was given the task of trying to help them divide up almost no assets, determine who would handle the children, and figure out how to take an impossibly meager salary under the best of situations and divide it for two households. It just does not work and I do not approve such irresponsible marriages".

"Til death do us part!" Death is so permanent and divorce so effortless.

ASSUMPTIONS

1. Marriage is too easily arranged.
2. Divorce likewise is made too easy.
3. Children are too often the product of very unsatisfactory unions at too young an age.
4. Too frequently the concept of "romantic love" overbalances "logical love" in terms of marriages and family.
5. Most women with a little motivation are bright enough to count to twenty; "a pill a day will keep the stork away". Now there are five year inserts and morning after pills.
6. Last minute counseling to attempt to prevent a divorce is usually too little and too late.

REMEDIES FOR THE MALE/FEMALE DILEMMA

1. A course will be offered in one of the first years of high school, perhaps under the aegis of health education, covering family living, sex education, and parenting.
2. A marriage license will be more difficult to procure. A longer waiting period will be required, a pre-marital medical exam shall be mandated, and minimum cash reserves and income established. The license will cost more.
3. Premarital counseling will be required (paid for by

the marriage license fees).

4. A premarital agreement must be developed in conjunction with the counseling. This will hold true for first and subsequent marriages. The premarital agreement will cover (but not necessarily be limited to):

a. Whether or not the couple wishes to have children. If the couple cannot have children would they wish to adopt children? How many in either case?

b. Who in the family will procure employment? Who will keep the family "books"? Will the couple maintain separate and/or joint accounts?

c. Other topics such as: Will each agree to stay in good physical condition? Smoking? Level of drinking if any? With whom will they spend the holidays? How much would they plan to save? Will they share religious views? Who disciplines the children? Do they share sexual values? (How frequently would sex be projected?) Will they agree that neither will physically or verbally abuse the other? Would they agree to a mutual check- in time (such as 6 p.m.) whereby each knows where the other is and whether they will be home for dinner? How many times a week would there be a family meal? If both work, who shares which household duties?

(An aside: I am told that if one truly loved another, it would not be necessary to develop a premarital agreement since trust is involved. My response traditionally has been that if you trust and believe in the other, you will also respect the other to the point that you can codify premarital expectations. In other words reason AND romance should be involved.)

5. Divorce will be more difficult to procure. A higher fee will be assessed and the couple will have pre-divorce counseling and/ or mediation service.

6. A baby license will be required. (See Chapter 1)

7. If a child is born to an unmarried mother, the child
   will become a ward of the court until it is determined
   the mother can provide for the child. If not, the child
   will be placed in a foster home or orphanage (shades
   of the Gingrich plan).

(Sorry! I do not accept the "any mother is better than
no mother" rationale.)

CHAPTER 12
POLITICS

*A*merican politics has been a passion of mine since I was a small tyke on the prairie. In fact by 1940 at age twelve I had a "We Want Willkie" headquarters on our front porch. Unfortunately or perhaps fortunately since Franklin Roosevelt was a great president and wartime leader, our neighborhood did not carry enough weight to swing the overall election. Perhaps the problem was that it was Iowa and not Cook County in Illinois, for they have been known to effect outcomes in the political arena.

As a matter of fact, I have an ambivalent feeling, sort of a "love/hate" attitude, with politics. The frustrations, inequities, downright dishonesty, and even fear too often associated with the political process may keep the very best talents from seeking office. General Colin Powell, a natural if there ever was another of the Eisenhower mold, comes to mind. Much of the problem roots with "we, the people", for our demands are too often extremely unreasonable and our expectations ludicrous. In effect, we want "lower taxes and more government services", a Catch 22 of the highest order. Difficulty then follows in that there are those who promise to deliver on both counts.

A story is recounted of the young political newcomer

who was both brilliant and articulate. The old political pros thought they would trip him up by asking the question on where he stood on the issue of whether the world was flat or round. His response was to ask them where they stood. He said he was prepared to argue either way.

Former Congressman Martin Dies of Texas nailed the challenge for an office seeker. He believed that no matter how talented the candidate was, no matter how dedicated and concerned, unless he could win an election, all his ability would go to waste. With each congressman, as an example, representing hundreds of thousands of people, getting out the word on qualifications is very difficult. Campaigning is time consuming, grueling, and unbelievably expensive. It can destroy families and alienate friends, ravage savings accounts, develop power pangs and paranoia, and even threaten the baby's milk money. When the fever hits a candidate, it can be all consuming and potentially self-destructive.

Yet, if the nation is to survive the complex challenges of the new millennium, we need even better qualified candidates to step forward.

Among the major misapprehensions running amok in the land is that we live in a democracy. This has not been true for centuries although semblances remain where town hall meetings actually vote for community policies. We live in a representative democracy or republic where we vote for a person to represent us. Once elected he or she must vote his/her own conscience and they might disagree with us even if they are in our party. If they are in the opposing party it is even more likely they will vote contrary to our wishes. That does not mean the elected official cannot take polls to determine the wishes of constituents. It means the official is not required to follow the wishes of his constituents. Obviously elected officials should be aware of the views of the people or their term in office is likely to be extremely short.

In my neighboring community, a city council member was threatened with recall because he voted on an issue for the good of all the city which, in the eyes of some of his constituents, negatively impacted his own ward.

We understand that in most athletic contests there is a winner and a loser. In some political campaigns a large number of people may be running which ultimately allows a winner (or a few winners if there are multiple seats of office at stake), but many losers. Elections are expensive processes in the staging thereof. With fewer elections, money is saved, but representative democracy not always served. For example in many partisan primary elections, to reach the party candidate to proceed to the general election against the other party, usually primary winner takes all is the ground rule. If you would like to impact the results, encourage multiple candidates with similar points of view to run against the single candidate of your differing point of view, and normally your viewpoint, even it is far in the minority, will prevail.A one on one runoff of the top two candidates from the primary would solve this dilemma, but it would be time consuming and expensive.

As a specific example, I remember some years ago when I ran for the congress as a Republican in a new district in Orange County, California. I was the unofficial candidate of the party as a result of a caucus (officially the parties may not endorse in contested primaries), but five GOP candidates still determined to run for office in the June primary. Four of us were moderate conservatives, and the fifth a rather radical conservative. Guess who won the contest? The votes ran roughly 18,000, 14,000, 7,000, 6,000, and 5,000. Although the analysis is too simple, in a runoff the vote could have been 32,000 to 18,000. Incidentally in the losing group were two lawyers who could profit from the advertising, otherwise prohibited to them at that time.

If you are still into the wondering mode, guess who won that general congressional seat election and held the office for a number of years until he went to jail in the infamous Koreagate scandal? If you guessed the Democrat, you are right, because the Republican party rank and file voter could not support that sense of extremism.

It takes money to run; at the turn of the new century big money will be required. Recently a Democratic congressman in Oregon opted to retain his seat in the congress rather than run for an open senatorial seat, because he was having trouble raising the dollars necessary, and a millionaire had already announced he was running for the Democratic party nomination. We have seen the impact of a Ross Perot who could influence political thought with some creative ideas AND millions of dollars as well. Steve Forbes, with almost no political background, quickly became a big time though unsuccessful player in the presidential sweepstakes. Money does not guarantee a win; Nelson Rockefeller and Barry Goldwater found that out, but it did not hurt Jack Kennedy, nor did his wealthy Ivy league supporters.

Nevertheless, communication costs a fortune today. Television, radio, newspaper advertising, and the direct mail expenses are staggering! The federal government slipped in a rather neat package to enable income tax payers to have a dollar deducted from their returns (now up to $3) for presidential candidates that meet certain requirements. In recent years the percentage of tax payers who have opted to give this small change (which totals millions in the aggregate) has become smaller and smaller.

Party primaries and caucuses start earlier and earlier which means campaigns last longer and longer. "Mean spirited" (a term I do not care for, but it may be appropriate here), negative advertising seems to offend voters and provides the other party with magnificent rhetoric from fellow primary candidates with which to cream the survivor at the general election. Ronald Reagan introduced an eleventh commandment for political candidates to "speak not ill of thy fellow party opponent" philosophy, seemingly wasted in recent campaigns.

Many political observers were nonplused when the presidential election winner in 1992 received less than 50 percent of the votes cast. Part of the reason was the presence of a serious third party candidate, but many citizens are turned off by candidates or conceivably do not consider themselves adequately informed to vote intelligently. That, in effect, would show good judgment in itself, and Americans should remember that not voting is an option we have. One hundred percent voting usually occurs only in totalitarian states.

Oregon recently introduced voting by mail which is very convenient and less expensive than manning polling places. It also introduces controversy as to just how easy should it be to vote, and whether others can control the votes of home voting citizens. Of course, absentee voting has been around for some time, and in a few states a high percentage of voters invariably opt to vote by mail even when in town, so it may well be an idea of merit.

Obviously the computer age has made maintaining voter lists if not vote tabulating much easier, and it should result in fewer human errors in counting ballots.

In most states a voter's pamphlet is published whereby not only are candidates listed, but they are also given the option of printing a campaign statement at a reasonable cost which serves as a partial offset to the wealthy candidate who deluges homes with his or her propaganda.

The issue of term limits is before the land as the century ends. Many states have taken action to control the limits of their elected state officials, but the US Constitution determines federal office term limits. It is another concept which appeals to the electorate, and just as the presidential term limit is set (the 22nd amendment), so can and should congressional and possibly federal judge terms be limited.

Another interesting phenomenon has received impetus in the latter years of the twentieth century: the use of the initiative and referendum to change laws. The amazing Proposition 13 passed by the voters of California to control property taxes (and create great challenges for local and state government) proved that citizens can indeed demand and bring about change. In effect democracy can still be heard. There is a concern that there may be too many initiatives placed on ballots which in turn can confuse voters. We shall see.

The impact of special interests and lobbyists on the political process is undergoing great scrutiny. This in turn is part of the "money" problem, and relates to Congressman Dies comment about the highest priority is winning before a candidate can do "good things". Very few Political Action Committees or lobbyists or even well heeled citizens do not have a pointed interest in issues that influence them. This may be in conflict with the good of the majority of the citizenry. Limiting contributions to campaigns seemingly has become a bipartisan issue. Visualize the pressure on a representative from North Carolina by the tobacco industry or on a candidate from Iowa by a farm crop subsidy group. When does the national good take precedence over the home state good (and don't forget who elects "you")?

Why do so many lawyers run for office? Obviously the nature of the profession, of making "laws" has to do with the law. Is it a good thing? Not necessarily. What can be done about it?

Federal office holders have awarded themselves a marvelous pension plan. In the 1996 primaries candidate Allen Keyes proposed putting them all on social security limits. He felt with that in mind, the log jam over how to resolve the potential and ultimate insolvency of social security would receive a high attention span and congressional action.

There must be an infinite number of outstanding citizens who would make excellent citizen legislators. Hopefully, offsetting a negative as to why term limits would not work, a citizen of reasonable "smarts" can find the rest rooms in less than two or four or six years. We must encourage good people to run for office, knowing that not everyone will win. The rank and file citizenry should be willing to put some dollars behind their candidates so a few people with big dollars do not control the game.

ASSUMPTIONS
1. Americans believe in their system of government.
2. We all want to see good candidates and intelligent, concerned people elected to office.
3. We also believe that government should be efficient as well as effective.
4. One should not have to be wealthy in order to run for office.

REMEDIES FOR POLITICAL CONCERNS
1. Term limits shall become effective for all political office holders who otherwise hold a tremendous power through incumbency. Term limits of six to twelve years in office would enable America to preserve and strengthen its belief in citizen legislators.
2. Runoffs should be held in party primaries.
3. The formal time period of running for office, filing and fund raising, should be reduced.
4. The media should continue to show fair play and extend equal time for opposing candidates.
5. Candidates must be willing to open their personal financial records for scrutiny.
6. Strict limitations should be placed on PACS, lobbies and individuals in terms of campaign contributions.

Public records should be made of individuals and groups donating more than $100 to campaigns (often done currently).

7. The usage of campaign funds by candidates should be better regulated. Giving away surplus funds or using them for personal expenses or postretirement spending should be eliminated.

CHAPTER 13
MINORITIES IN AMERICA

Over the past two centuries the United States of America has become known as the international "melting pot". Native son status necessarily must be reserved for "Native Americans" or American Indians if we use a pure definition of just who was here first. In terms of numbers, they have become a minority statistic and a rather embarrassing statistic since their treatment has been shabby at best. Now thanks to the national movement toward gaming centers their economic plight has improved markedly; in fact, becoming as much as one- sixteenth Pequot can guarantee a comfortable income.

When national commentary centers on minorities, the parallel phrase of consequence is "discrimination". A minority can be a racial, religious, political, sexual, nationality, age, height, weight, physical condition (here's where a judicious use of etc, etc applies) grouping. There is probably no "group" against which some discrimination does not exist, and I submit today in the USA the group most maligned may be the WASP (white, anglo-saxon protestant) male. We have even had membership in formerly all male organizations such as Rotary forced into coed status. The good news is that I recently met a man who had joined the Soroptimst club (which by basic definition has to do with sisters). The PEO is holding out as is the Daughters of the American Revolution (who refer male applicants to Sons of the American Revolution).

A zillion laws have been placed on the books to prevent discrimination against as many minorities as possible. Indeed, one should not discriminate, and may not in terms of jobs, housing, and select other categories. I would defend the right of one to discriminate volubly in the sanctity of his or her broom closet. A South Dakotan might rail against the injustices heaped on him by North Dakotans or we MacGregor clan members might rue the injustices of the crown and the Campbell clan.

So some discrimination, "come on Trojans, down with the Fighting Irish", will exist in the land. It's the negative economic and social consequences of which we must rightly be concerned.

I will never forget the discrimination shown against two of my Caucasian friends who were ranking administrators in the school system in Hawaii a number of years ago. They were in line for top jobs, but then realized that they were minority members in Hawaii as WASPS. In effect the nisei controlling majority wanted one of their own as "top gun" and so it happened. My associates were very positive about the reality of the situation and both procured excellent school administrative jobs back in California. Even today if a WASP wants to see what it feels like to be a minority person he or she might spend time in the 50th state.

There are more members of the Roman Catholic Church than any other religious denomination in the United States. Yet, there are more protestants of all denominations than Roman Catholics. Is there discrimination against Roman Catholics? Probably by narrow minded individuals, and this will still be true as the century turns. In 1960 there was genuine concern as to whether a Roman Catholic could be elected president of the United States until John Fitzgerald Kennedy proved the country was ready to judge the person, not his religion.

Over the centuries of this passing millennium, more excesses have taken place in the name of God than perhaps by any other force. In the middle ages the extremism of the inquisition created a blemish on mankind. The cruelty shown Huguenots, French protestants, as well as other religious injustices by religious extremists led thousands to seek religious freedom in this new land.

Even today maintaining a separation of church and state has been an incendiary issue in the nation. The impact of "true believers" in the election process can be marked, and biblical quotations or excerpts from the Koran can be used to form inflammatory opinions and excesses.

Perhaps the saddest commentary is that there are those with an organizational economic conflict of interest who profit from discrimination.

I do marvel at the identification of women as a minority for purposes of preventing discrimination just as I recognize there has been and is still a latent discrimination in employment opportunities and equal pay for equal jobs for women. It's just that there are more women than men which normally does not technically make women a minority group. Although 4 percent more boy babies are born, the weaker sex, the male, soon becomes the smaller number of surviving adults. (You can clearly see that women should be giving up their seats on buses and opening doors for this weaker sex. Should anyone doubt the logic, look at life expectancy tables).

Using the analogy of the school business, I was invariably amazed to see that custodians usually were on a higher salary schedule than secretaries, and anyone with a limited but realistic view of who makes things happen in schools as well as many businesses knows that secretaries are the hidden power behind the scene. Early on though custodians were men and secretaries were women which justified the difference. In fact in the thirties women teachers were expected to be single, and if they were married they could lose their jobs.

Now the "killer" point. Yielding the viewpoint that efforts are still needed to assure equal opportunities between males and females and there is no room for sexual harassment in our society, we have made vast progress for all minorities and should be aware of that crucial point. There are those who profit from insisting that discrimination is as bad or worse than ever.

This is especially true in the area of racial groupings. Yes, there are areas of discrimination, and now reverse discrimination, but if anyone cannot see progress since 1940 I would be concerned about a major conflict of interests. There have been no slaves in the land since the end of the Civil War in 1865 well over a century ago. No living person has been a slave and few if any have had parents who were slaves even as infants. Yet a slave mentality exists in some people who use this as an excuse for poor behavior or poor job performance or a poor work ethic. I was very impressed with Jesse Jackson when he exhorted blacks to stop complaining and work hard to improve their lives

By almost every standard Black Americans have made great progress as an ethnic group since 1940. Most obvious and viewable are their successes in athletics and show business, but the black middle class has burgeoned as have their numbers in professions across the land. Yet there are those prophets of doom and gloom who push the party line that blacks have no chance in America today. Worse, there are those who know better yet feel they must accept this party line.

Is America still the land of opportunity for all? I would like to believe so. Again using the school analogy, look at the parents of a number of immigrant students, many non-English speaking boat families having emerged from the horror and the chaos of the Vietnam War in Southeast Asia. They worked hard in this new (to them) land, and eventually owned a business. Frequently their children became high school valedictorians.

Language has been a barrier for so many, and our nation has bent over backward to help newcomers. In theory one must be reasonably competent in English to become a citizen. Then why are we printing ballots in multiple languages? Those responsible for bilingual education have major disagreements as to whether courses should be taught in English and all students placed in crash "English" courses, or taught in native tongues as English is gradually learned on the side.

We may have left a critical point regarding racial relations. Are more blacks incarcerated than whites? Undoubtedly "yes" on a percentage of population basis. There are a number of reasons why this is so. Since most contemporary prison populations reflect the drug culture, crack cocaine used by more blacks is considered a worse problem than regular cocaine ingested by the white society. Moreover, more black children are born into poverty, into a single parent environment. Today 70 percent of black births are to unmarried, mostly very young mothers. Whites should not be complacent since 30 percent of white births are to unmarried mothers. Nevertheless, we are almost guaranteeing a life of crime to many of those children born with limited hope. The good news is that some of those youngsters will overcome the odds and become success stories.

The subject of immigration is also perplexing in the waning years of the twentieth century. Almost all Americans are immigrants or related to immigrants. Moreover, many of the Western states need immigrant Hispanic farm labor (while the national unemployment rate hovers at 5 to 6 percent, many of whom may not be employable). Yet politicians are conjecturing on erecting huge fences or digging deep ditches to keep out the immigrants. We may have come within an eyelash of encouraging the immigration of most of Haiti a few years ago.

World population growth and the concomitant starvation which too often results will also have an impact on the United States. When you see world population projections of seventeen billion by the year 2150, early in the millennium, it gives one pause to worry about our great-great-great grandchildren. What we do today influences their ultimate world, if indeed the world survives. Let's be positive and assume the world will survive, so now our task is to make it workable as we re-orient challenges. (Do you believe the dinosaurs thought there would always be a tomorrow for themselves?)

Another contemporary concern is sexual orientation of many of our citizens. Apparently homosexuality is ages old, but in recent years the subject has been polarized. Our nation has difficulty ascertaining what number of homosexuals exists. For years, the number 10 percent of the population was used. A gay baseball umpire wrote a book and expressed the belief that 15 to 20 percent was a better number, while recent excursions into census research brought the figure to a 2 1/2 percent figure. No one seems to know why people are homosexual although there is a heated difference of opinion among gays as to whether it is a matter of choice or biological selection.

Is it possible for homosexuals to be treated as every day citizens? In terms of their rights, absolutely. Beyond that it depends on how they wish to be perceived in society. Witnessing the Gay Rights Parade in San Francisco is enough to discourage many heterosexuals who prefer to see sort of a common level of behavior among all citizens. In other words, drawing attention to oneself, and then saying now ignore me, may be counterproductive.

Whether gay couples should have marital rights is another challenging issue. Historically marriage has had much to do with producing children, a goal not generally sought by gay couples. Why should gay couples receive more rights, insurance benefits as an example, than heterosexual couples who choose not to be formally married but elect to live together as life partners?

Age discrimination is yet another major issue in our society. Seniors are hardly a minority, and most citizens will arrive there at some point. Now it is difficult to identify when the appellation "senior citizen" legitimately begins. The American Association of Retired People (AARP) will start enrolling people at 50. By 65 most senior discounts apply. Being old is largely a head trip, and some choose never to play the game. As a matter of fact, if social security is to survive much beyond the beginning of the millennium, senior citizenship may have to commence at 70 or 75 if most folks will be living into their nineties.

How about discriminating against pudgy people? We have recently been told that about 74 percent of us are overweight, so the group is in the clear majority. Slender people be prepared for discrimination!

In recent years Congress has passed the Americans with Disabilities Act. Mental and physical disabilities are perhaps the most obvious of handicaps. Most people of good faith accept others and are willing to aid them when appropriate and accept their strengths and positive contributions to our society. Still our schools have a special challenge to develop understanding among all peoples.

It seems that coming back to the role of schools is a recurrent theme. The schools already have a rich agenda of "must dos"; yet no other institution reaches almost all of our citizens for a number of their formative years. A talented, honest, aware teacher may be the best remedy for the ill of discrimination in our future society.

ASSUMPTIONS

1. All people are NOT created equal other than in the eyes of God.
2. In the United States of America we are basically guaranteed equal rights and broad opportunities. Still the differences between people will provide different outcomes in our lives.
3. Humans learn to discriminate against others. A song lyric reminds us, "They have to be carefully taught". Children innately are open.
4. Each person must be aware that he or she is a member of some minority in our society and there will be those who are unkind to us.
5. Each person also has the ability to develop tolerance toward others and acceptance of the invaluable difference between human beings.
6. Although there are many shortcomings in our society, opportunities for all minorities have shown improvement over the years. Progress is being made, and to deny this is to succumb to a new form of reverse prejudice or discrimination.

REMEDIES FOR PROBLEMS REGARDING MINORITIES

1. English must become America's primary language. All official documents must be in English alone. Schools will teach in English, and English will be presented as a primary subject until students of a foreign tongue reach a basic level of fluency in English.
2. We must each respect our own cultural heritage and preserve our ties to our diverse culture.
3. Artificial quotas based on race, sex or age should not be used for hiring or college entrance proceedings. However, employers should be mindful of the desirabil-

ity of having a balanced work force and voluntarily seek qualified employees from minority groups. The courts apparently are minimizing affirmative action.

4. Future teachers should be given sensitivity training in their "methods" of teaching courses.

5. Sensitivity training and awareness of discrimination should be encompassed in school units from grade one and emphasis added by eighth and eleventh grade US history and senior government courses.

CHAPTER 14
INTERNATIONAL RELATIONS

*A*merica! The great melting pot of mankind. Almost everyone's family, at some time, immigrated to the United States. We were an upstart nation for well over our first century as a United States. By the conclusion of World War II in 1945, before our bicentennial celebration, we were the preeminent nation in the world. Earlier in the century, just prior to World War I, we wanted to pull up our drawbridge and be left alone. No entangling alliances for the United States! No siree!

How it happened is history. Where it will take us has yet to be determined. What we do know is that no one can analyze current issues before the United States and not look at our status as world leader. Forget the fact that we are head over heels in debt and do not seem to be able to balance our own national budget. Forget the fact that our currency has had a rocky ride against the German mark and Japanese yen in recent years. Ignore our extremely negative balance of international trade. Uncle Sam remains the sugar daddy of the world. Count on it!.

We have before us a challenge and an opportunity. We are in position to lead the world into an era of unprecedented opportunity. There seem to be no major adversaries who could propel the world into war as witnessed twice in the twentieth century. Cooperation in the world, by and large, seems positive. Communication, transportation, and manufacturing are stable and our nation has been pledged through NAFTA to cooperate even more fully with our neighbors.

Occasionally the United States embarks on a " holier than thou" trip preaching the gospel of human rights to all nations; forgetting that we have more than a few skeletons in our own back yard.

The United Nations is working, even with an inflated staff and budget, and our collective efforts to enforce world security also holds promise.

Somehow we continue to search for peace in the Mideast where terrorism is a way of life. Even the civilized British have not resolved problems in the empire. The ethnic differences in Yugoslavia may carry on for more years as will struggles in India, Iraq, Turkey, Greece and Cypress. In many countries guns appear to be the route to capture and control "power", that five letter word that has enslaved so much of mankind. Africa remains a quandary wrapped in the classical enigma, and chaos only a crop failure or a tribe away.

A critical matter is raw material, and current estimates indicate that by the middle of the next century, with barely a dent in the millennium, many vital commodities such as oil will be in short supply. However, new reserves invariably crop up, and technological efforts to provide alternate forms of energy are proceeding beyond drawing boards. Even the old nemesis of nuclear energy can offer a clarion call, if only we could fathom how many fathoms deep we should bury the hazardous waste, another major example of the NIMBY experience ("not in my back yard").

Population control is desperately needed and flying in

the face of certain religious convictions. The five to six billions on the planet will double soon enough, and still the US of A with about 5 percent of the world's population utilizes a high percentage of the world's raw materials. The good news on the population front is that even the African's family size is decreasing. The bad news is that still represents six children or so per family. The Chinese seem to have a grasp on population control, and we offer them lessons on human rights. What a paradox.

The "have not" nations of the world, the so called third world nations, can see what "goods" are available to the rich of the world. The view is as close as the televisions that abound almost everywhere. The world over, folks can sit in their living room (loll in the oasis?) and watch man be inhumane to man. Who's fighting whom today? They also see goods and services to dream about. Only when a nation can develop a strong middle class does it seem to achieve a desirable stability.

There is still evil abroad notwithstanding the collapse of the soviet union with its threat of world communism. Missiles remain "at large", the removal of which from the world scene must be a high priority. There are also those including Iraq who may yet be toying with biological warfare weaponry.

Still the new century, the start of the new millennium, offers hope unparalleled for mankind. How we handle the opportunity, especially as Americans, is a critical step to the future. Informed citizenry, willing and ready to contribute positive ideas for those many tomorrows, will make the difference.

ASSUMPTIONS
1. The United States is now the military, economic and probably moral leader of the world.
2. Nevertheless, the United Nations is the common meeting place for the world's autonomous nations.

3. The Security Council of the UN should be able to handle the basic military disputes between nations and problems of international security.
4. Terrorism continues to threaten relationships throughout the world.
5. High level, rapid and candid communication can be maintained.
6. Enmity between nations and factions within nations based on historical ethnic, political, and religious differences must be recognized. It will not go away.
7. Many nations still need to take more positive steps toward population control.
8. Nations given good information can become responsible in terms of ecological and environmental balance.

REMEDIES FOR INTERNATIONAL CONCERNS

1. Clearly a strong effort should be made by world nations to recognize and accept the obvious; English is the most common world language.
2. Although our support of the United Nations, conceived and located in the United States, must continue at a high level, we must never relinquish our national sovereignty to a One World Government.
3. The world of nations must continue to put pressure on to overcome historic enmities between nations and segments of nations. We cannot tolerate this interfracidal strife that could threaten if not world then at least regional peace.
4. The United States must put its own house in order to be worthy of the responsibility and challenge of world leadership. This includes paying off our national debt, balancing our budget, promoting human rights in the US, overcoming the drug scene, and strengthening the moral fiber of the land so that children do not beget children, especially out of wedlock.

5. We must demand that other nations of the world assume stronger shared responsibility in meeting the economic burdens of world peace and prosperity. We do not have the resources to support all of the world.
6. Although the United States should encourage human rights for all nations, especially through precept and example, we must put our own house in order. We must also respect the sovereign rights of other nations even as we disagree with them as long as there is no threat to the United States or to world peace.
7. We must encourage nations to control their populations, and we should provide information and technology to help them.
8. Combatting world terrorism must be a high priority for the USA and United Nations.
9. International cooperation must be increased to control the world drug scene.
10. We must encourage all nations to respect the frail ecological balance of the world, but we must also understand their needs. Reason and balance must apply.

CHAPTER 15
GENERAL
ISSUES

*V*ery few current issues stand alone; that is, there is invariably overlap in greater or lesser degree. Homelessness generally may be categorized with poverty and in recent years with mental health since so many homeless would have been institutionalized but a few years ago. Poverty also correlates with consumer economic education since it is not always how much money is available for a family or individual to spend, but how the money is apportioned out.

Obviously money spent in gambling, buying cigarettes, alcohol or drugs will not be available for the first and last month's deposit on a rental unit, or for a down payment on a home, nor, of course, for baby shoes or milk. It is also cheaper to bake a pie than to buy a ready-made pie, and it is cheaper invariably (or should be) to eat at home than to dine out, even at the golden arches. However, we have looked at consumer economic education, and realize that most people should commit themselves to reforming their spending habits.

The point is that this chapter will encompass some repetition of earlier topics, problems and remedies.

So many of our concerns are attitudinal and not necessarily economic. A few homeless people would rather be on the street than in shelters. If one is hooked on drugs or booze or even cigarettes, logic as to spending priorities is thrown out the window, subordinated to habit or need. The "fix" is the thing!

The issue of medical assistance stands out. There is a clear need for everyone to have health insurance or care. People fit into perhaps three or four categories. First is the person who is covered on the job as is his or her family. How important it is for a young person looking at a career to understand the meaning of the term "fringe benefits", foremost of which is a health plan. Then there is the person who has no company sponsored health plan, but who incorporates a basic health insurance program into his/her budget. That may mean giving up other things—dining out, smoking, drinking, even a second car in a family setting, or a nice vacation. Choices must be made! Next there is the person who just claims not to have the money for insurance so they go uninsured or depend on welfare or free health programs.Finally seniors over 65 have Medicare and hopefully the fairly inexpensive medigap coverage.

An emerging issue adds to the discussion. My own experiences with HMOs (health maintenance organizations) has been very positive, and my insurance premiums were markedly cut as a result. However, there are those, including numerous medical doctors, who rap the HMO concept. In some cases where one is not assigned a specific doctor or does not have choice, there could be problems, of course. I have seemingly always had a choice. I do have to work with a primary care physician who does not play give away, but eventually works with me as to special needs. A co-payment is required, but I strongly favor such an individual commitment. If I am not ill enough to dedicate some of my resources to paying a small part of the care, then I probably should not be going to the doctor.

Whether we will ever have a national health plan is debatable. Americans who oppose a national health plan look to other countries (Canada, England) for horror stories. Those who favor a national health plan look to other countries (Canada, England) for their success stories. Apparently success or failure is in the eye of the beholder.

A critical question remains as the point (usually an age) whereby public tax money or any mutual benefit health plan should cease financing heroic and extremely expensive measures to prolong the ultimate. Death is inevitable. Should a heart replacement be made at age 100? The embarrassing part for me is my ambivalence. If I were a multi-millionaire and wanted to pay for my own heart transplant at age 100, should I be allowed to do so? Hearts and other organs as replacement parts are in short supply. What are the legalities and the ethics involved in this great basically free enterprise society of ours? Is the supply of organs a variable in the equation?

Go a step further. Suppose I am on welfare or medicare. At what age does my right to a heart transplant end? How about kidney dialysis? An appendectomy? A hang nail?

Perhaps it is easier to consider a non-controversial issue. How about abortion? This has been the most divisive issue in the United States for a number of years. Chapter one in this book considers a radical approach, but short of that, what are the options? Since the majority believes in freedom of choice, a political candidate who favors pro-life, if he or she is foolish enough to take a definitive stand, should lose.

That does not make pro-choice right. The ludicrous thing is that it should be a nonissue or an extremely minor one. If a woman decides to become sexually active, there are many relatively secure birth control devices foremost of which is the pill. However, it apparently requires the client to be able to count to twenty and take appropriate action. Currently we have a "monthly" pill, a five year implant, and now a morning after pill. Why did this no brainer become such a big issue? We are back to attitudes and welfare or search for "love" or whatever a psychologist might ante up for an excuse for sexual irresponsibility.

Then there is a gun control. Now that world communism no longer threatens an invasion of our households, we need new bogeymen. Crime in the streets and carried to our doorsteps is not bad as a replacement unit. However, the statistic that shooting a family member or friend with household weapons is 43 times more likely to happen than shooting an invader seems to make no impact. "If we take away our weapons, only criminals will have guns!" goes another argument.

If we can enforce the "third crime, do time" law, we should be able to figure out how to incarcerate bad people carrying or otherwise possessing guns. One of the points of this book is for a citizen to be active in supporting their viewpoint, possibly by affiliating with a forceful group of people. The National Rifle Association is a case point as a group that makes things, not necessarily desirable things, happen. The ACLU and Trial Lawyers Association are also potent forces, often at loggerheads one group against the other.

In recent years the subject of child and spousal abuse has loomed large in our society. Corporal punishment in schools or even the home encourages debate. There is such a thing as verbal abuse, but our laws seem to follow the old adage of "sticks and stones can break my bones, but words can never hurt me". Child support is another contentious issue. It seems that computers and social security numbers make possible the location of all citizenry, as "big brother" as that sounds. My philosophy is that as long as I have nothing to hide (well, maybe a few tiny, personal things), my phone number and address are not exactly sacred trusts. One must pay the piper. If we make marrying tougher and have baby licenses mandated, we will have far fewer child support cop outs.

The auto, the most expensive toy we Americans give ourselves (in an aggregate sense and over a life time, the costs of cars will far exceed our investment in homes, which often appreciate—rarely does a car gain value in the average person's ownership tenure) creates problems. Carnage (interesting word stem) on the highway exceeds casualties in wars. Higher speeds create more carnage; yet, we have shot down rational speed limits to favor two dimensional pursuit of the wild blue yonder. Our infrastructure (in this case meaning highways) is becoming unglued; a major challenge for the new century. AMTRAK is in trouble and public transportation needs a boost. When the transmission of my car went out recently, for the first time in years I was "forced" to take the regional bus line. It was surprisingly good.

In categories such as the local "Mom and Pop" store or transportation, even though prices may be higher or it may be inconvenient to ride a bus, we should support the systems to insure their survival. Let's call this a "remedy" and place it at the end of the chapter. In fact, let's end the chapter with one final topic.

Hopefully an idea whose time is long overdue, can be strengthened as we proceed into the next century. The concept of "Random Acts of Kindness" is supported by every positive thing we have ever heard including the basic Golden Rule "Do unto others as you would have them do unto you". "Love your neighbor as yourself" must also be a rallying cry for this simple, yet noble idea. Two of America's classiest home spun psychologists and philosophers, and fellow Iowans, Ann Landers and Dear Abby have led the charge for this movement. Oprah and others have promoted the concept.

ASSUMPTIONS

1. Problems can be solved—by individuals willing to accept responsibility for themselves. However, there are those who cannot help themselves for whom our compassion must be shown.
2. Likewise government should not be an enemy. We the people elect the government; we must abide by our rules; we are able to change the rules; and if necessary we must be willing to serve as elected officials.
3. Things don't just happen; someone makes them happen. It could be you.
4. We have the resources to help the genuinely needy, preferably through the private sector—The Salvation Army and Goodwill for openers among so many others, and for housing—Habitat for Humanity. The name of the game is people helping people.
5. We have an exemplary system of public education (and private schools as well for those who so choose). Our schools can "move over" if their constituents emphasize a special need. In other words the curriculum, beyond state dictates, is determined by "local rule".
6. Often in our society the careless, indifferent, and the irresponsible are rewarded (through welfare, free legal service, free medical care as examples). Nevertheless, virtue continues to be its own reward.

REMEDIES FOR GENERAL ISSUES

1. "Charity begins at home". We should take care of our own families, then our neighbors, our church group, our communities, our counties and our state. The closer services are provided to the needy, the

better, more personal and dedicated the service. Furthermore, for every subsequent level of bureaucracy, there is an added cost. Keep welfare as close to home as possible.

2. Consumer economic education should be a mandatory subject in our schools.

3. We must commence a war on illegitimacy as we have on drugs. Whether we need another czar remains to be seen. Teenagers should be consulted and may show leadership as they have with Students Against Driving Drunk (SADD) and the "Just Say No to Drugs" program. A new program being encouraged by the wife of the governor of Oregon and others, STARS (Students Today Aren't Ready for Sex) is programmed to promote celibacy until marriage among teens.

4. Vouchers should not be promoted for private schools. It will further encourage a caste system and lower public school standards. To promote different interests, satellite, magnet, charter or special interest programs can be established in the public schools.

5. People must be encouraged to plan their retirement programs to supplement social security and to prepare for their possible need for "long term care".

6. Management of social security funds should have the option of investing in private sector securities.

7. Broader utilization of alternate day commuting should be encouraged. Drivers whose license numbers end in odd or even numbers would be allowed to drive into cities on alternate days. This will promote car pools and use of public transport.

8. FLEX schedules for workers should be increasingly utilized.

9. The computer age will also allow more and more people to work at home on the network as it were.

10. All medical service must receive some co-payment from the consumer to the provider to make aware a

"cost" for all services and discourage what otherwise might seem to be "free".

11. No corporal punishment will be used in schools. Instead students who misbehave will be penalized where it hurts most... through their time and money.

12. Social security numbers will be assigned at birth and all children will have one prior to starting into school. A DNA social security number ID program will be initiated, and only one number sanctioned for each person.

13. Gasoline taxes, earmarked for highway repair and construction, will be so utilized.

14. The concept of issuance of traffic tickets through radar and photo ID, advertised publicly, will be utilized. It is not a game out there (and I shall pay my fines if you will).

15. Consumers should shop close to home when possible to insure that goods and services remain available.

16. Americans should commit themselves to performing "Random Acts of Kindness". What a great country this will be!

CHAPTER 16
ACTIVIST CITIZENS

*I*f you have disagreed with some or a number of issues and remedies developed in this book, then both the reader and author have been partially successful. If you have been motivated to do something about the issues, we are even more successful. Remember in the English language "you" carries both a second person singular and plural connotation. Action to bring about constructive change, of course, can start with one person, but collective action has many advantages.

Adages abound to cover this challenge. "There is strength in numbers". "Many hands make light work" ad infinitum. In fact, old timers might conjure up the image of Nelson Eddy jauntily swinging down the road with his rousing chorus singing, "Give me some men who are stout hearted men . . ." and you will wind up with ten thousand more. To get things done it may take ten thousand more. Visualize the work to place an initiative proposition on a state ballot.

But, simply put, it starts with YOU (second person singular!)

The challenges may be obvious but are worth repeating. One must be aware of issues, people, places, happenings and events. This is not always easy when the thrust of contemporary society is toward entertainment, music TV, sports and six second sound bytes. Horror stories continue with reports on the woeful level of geographic and historical information on the part of too many citizens. As a history teacher, my orientation is that "the past is prelude", a building block for the tomorrows and tomorrows that will constitute the new century and new millennium. We can go back to that congressman, now a US senator who could not locate Bosnia after thousands of GIs had been sent there to preserve a fragile peace. (Let's give him a break and call it temporary campaign stress).

So one becomes aware of current issues by reading newspapers and books, listening to radio and watching TV newscasts and special reports, reading news magazines, and discussing contemporary events with friends and family. Ah, the family! How wonderful it would be if serious issues were brought up at the family dinner table and the children expected to be informed, even do some research on a special topic slated for a day or so in advance. Remember, this concept flies in the face of the fact that half our families are watching TV as they eat their meals. If it must happen, hopefully the shows are the news.

Being informed enables one to have enligthened opinions; suddenly one becomes political, and an activist is born.

Before pursuing the role of a committed activist, let's go back to a base point. Our most important task is our home base. If we lose sight of that, we may be damaging more than we are building. The aforementioned family dinners and other confabs can result in a cohesiveness, togetherness, and camaraderie that will engender loyalty and respect within the family. Hopefully there is a time for meditation; prayer for those who are so inclined. When the children are gone, then a husband and wife, if that is the status of the family, can become even closer by sharing opinions and feelings and goals.

Another variable within the family circle is nutrition and health. When three-quarters of Americans are overweight, family discussion on good health habits may be very important. Conceivably "bikes and hikes" will represent another form of togetherness.

Now that our average citizen has joined the ranks of the informed and desires to become an activist, let's say an "issues missionary", what can happen? Obvious possibilities include forming or joining existing information groups, book clubs, nature or environmental groups, political clubs and organization, civic groups, service clubs, church groups, even kaffee klatches. We can attend lectures, take college courses, go to elderhostels (with a sprinkling of white hair), go to town hall meetings, city council sessions, school board meetings ad infinitum.

Invite political office holders and candidates to your group's sessions. They love audiences; it's an inherent part of their psyche. Ask pointed questions. Accept a reasonable difference of opinion on some issues, but do not hesitate to disagree when it is important to you.

Thus far you have been spared my 95 percent theory. My contention is that too many people expect 100 percent "party line" loyalty. If a representative agrees 95 percent with one person's views, the 5 percent is too big a gap for that person's small mind to handle. Admittedly if vital issues are concerned there could be a valid problem, but some honest disagreement is probably good. As mentioned earlier in a community near my home, a city councilman was recalled because a vociferous few were upset with one vote which was to expand a controversial halfway house in their ward. Most agreed that overall he had a splendid record, and the council voted unanimously

on the issue. Of course, NIMBY was involved. A few hot
heads apparently believed that he should take a citizen's
vote to determine how the citizenry felt on each issue
before the council, but that is not how representative
government is supposed to work. With a few "town hall"
oriented exceptions our government is not a democracy
as has been pointed out, it is a representative republic.
We obey the laws until we change the laws, for the people
do have that power.

Years ago the "people's revolution" at the University
of California was led by a young man named Mario Savio.
My understanding of his basic philosophy is that a person need not obey laws with which they disagree. At what
price anarchy? Again if we disagree with specific laws, we
the people can bring about the needed change: no Adolph
Hitlers needed here.

The ultimate in citizen action is to actually seek office.
It may start out by being on a community advisory group
or committee or board. It may be jury duty. Obviously
someone has to serve as elected officials— city council
members and school boards. In many situations the pay
is limited to non-existent, the hours may be long, and
the task thankless. But good people are needed. Uncle
Sam needs us!

Then there is county government, the state legislature, and the national congress, and then the presidency.
Undoubtedly the office of President of the United States
is the most frustrating, challenging, difficult task that a
man (and ultimately a woman) can perform. The negative side of partisan politics is the contentious or
adversarial relationship deemed necessary. Franklin
Roosevelt gloated over the enemies he had made, for in
his opinion he had earned their enmity through doing
proper and needed tasks. "Enemy" is not my favorite
word, but is probably modest compared to some of the
invective used in campaigns.

Well, you may have decided not to run for the presidency today or tomorrow, but you can support citizens with whom you mostly agree in their campaigns. Volunteer your time and money and encouragement. On issues you can write letters to the editor, take out ads, print up your views as handouts, and, of course, vote. Each of us can be heard and make something happen. We will not win them all, but we might cause positions to move toward our views, the proper views, of course.

A discourse on citizen action should not take place in the late twentieth century without reference to two men, now both deceased, Howard Jarvis and Paul Gann. These men developed an organization to support a cause, property tax relief in California, which was known as Proposition 13. Later such movements spread throughout the nation as grass roots efforts. As a school administrator at the time, I opposed it, but retrospectively I believe it had to happen, for governments and their operators, the politicians and the staffs, had almost carte blanche at raising taxes for the purpose of supporting if not expanding government. A close friend in Southern California, a teacher, told me she had to support Proposition 13 because in the next year the taxes on her home would have been raised $2500 a year.

Thousands upon thousands of people were enlisted in this struggle for property tax relief and it worked. The legislators were not about to take action. Likewise in more recent times, many states have passed term limits for their legislators. Career politicians would rarely take a stand to remove themselves from office.

There are those who claim we have too many propositions on our ballots that make it difficult for voters to be informed, are costly, and conceivably destructive in philosophy. Amending the federal constitution is a rather difficult task, but in the case of term limits for federal office holders, it might have to happen. Occasionally mistakes are made, or situations change. Obviously the 18th amendment or prohibition in 1919 was undone by the 21st amendment in 1933.

We the people have the right to petition and to make laws if our office holders cannot lead the way to what the majority perceive as a needed change. Recall is also a possibility, but it must be used responsibly. The basic point is any one of us, serving in office, is expendable. There is no such thing as an indispensable office holder, and change is inevitable (although a few 90 plus year old senators seem to have pleased their constituents almost indefinitely).

Two thoughts in closure. First is the well known "serenity prayer"

> *"Oh, God give me the serenity to accept that which I cannot change,*
> *The courage to change that which I can change,*
> *And the wisdom to know the difference."*

Finally a paraphrase on some well known advice.

> *"I am only one person,*
> *but I am one person.*
> *I cannot do everything,*
> *but I can do some things.*
> *I do have opinions,*
> *but new information may alter them.*
> *I am responsible for myself,*
> *but I can have a positive influence on my family and friends.*
> *I cannot change the entire world,*
> *but I can help make a small part of the world a better place in which to live"*

All of this for the century and the millennium to come.

APPENDIXES

APPENDIX A
FUTURING: FORECASTING THE FUTURE

*W*e have a recorded history of the past, a fairly good grasp on the present, but the future is something of an open book. The end of a century and the millennium is the perfect time for speculating on the future. In effect, one can assume what future events "will be". The best prognosis for what "will be" is a continuum of what is being and has been just rolled forward. Prognosticators, depending on their level of optimism or pessimism, might issue their views on what could happen down the line in best case and worst case scenarios. Hopefully a futurist is able to assimilate from the areas of sociology, psychology and technology to project what "should be" in the future. Some of the remedies suggested in this book would markedly alter a status quo projection for future years.

To be candid, as this book is being written, there is technically no verb for "futuring" although there undoubtedly will be. The term is occasionally used nevertheless, and there are perfectly good nouns as "future" and "futurist".

There is also a World Future Society which was founded

in 1966 and based in Bethesda, Maryland (7910 Woodmont Avenue, Suite 450, Bethesda, MD 20814) which describes itself as "An Association for the Study of Alternative Futures". This organization issues a periodical, *The Futurist*, which is "A Journal of forecasts, trends and ideas about the Future." The Society also develops opportunities for face to face learning experiences including general assemblies, conferences and seminars.

In effect futurists do not predict the future since the future is not predictable. Futurists try to propose what might happen in the future. By anticipating what might happen or even more significant, what should happen in an idealistic sense, better planning can take place. Literally the future can be changed by humans working together. Existing technology can be advanced.

An example of the future being markedly altered took place in the few years after President John F. Kennedy suggested in the early 1960s that we should place a man on the moon by the end of the decade of the sixties. Goal setting was matched by an emphasis in the technology involved, and the US placed a man on the moon in 1969. That was "the great step for mankind".

Scientists, indeed, are making plans for the future and forecasting what may be possible if not probable. For example Stephen Millett and William Kopp of the Battelle Research Institute in Columbus, Ohio, listed ten top innovative products which could be on hand in the year 2006. Their report was made in the July-August 1996 issue of *The Futurist*.

1. *Genetaceuticals*. This will be developed by combining genetic research with the reaction of pharmaceutical companies. Areas which might be impacted include cystic fibrosis, A.L.S. (Lou Gehrig's disease), multiple sclerosis, osteoporosis, and Alzheimer's disease.
2. *Personalized computers*. This innovation would be mobile and versatile as its user.

3. *Multi-fuel automobiles.* Future cars may run on two or more separate fuels.
4. *Next-generation television* which would interact with other computers and allow videoconferencing at home tying the home and office closer together.
5. *Electronic cash.* Debit cards will be further advanced and encompass house keys, driver's licenses, medical records and more.
6. *Home health monitors.* They will represent the live- in medical team.
7. *Smart maps and tracking devices.*
8. *Smart materials.* Such material as in buildings and highways might change color when they are no longer safe.
9. *Weight control and anti aging products.*
10. *Never owned products.* Leasing will be the future mode for those products whose technological change is rapid.

A decade is a rather short range for projections and obviously, there are no guarantees. As a point of interest, in 1982 *The Futurist* magazine gained permission to reprint an article from The *Ladies Home Journal* of December 1900 when they listed what may happen in the twentieth century.

They missed in projecting a population in the U.S.A of from 350 to 500 million, but accurately reported that Americans would be taller by an inch or so. They also stated the letters C, X and Q would no longer be used in our everyday alphabet (they missed). Their belief there would be no more flies or mosquitos was also over optimistic. However, they predicted ready cooked meals (if frozen dinners count). Coal would not be used for heating and cooking and this is largely true. Street cars would be disappearing from the larger cities, but instead they disappeared from the smaller towns and still are used in major cities here and there. Fast trains and telephotos were projected as was the demise of the horse drawn carriage. Air ships were foreseen three years before the Wright Brothers flew. The *Journal* article forecast television, a hit; and strawberries as large as apples, a miss.

What will happen the next century let alone in the coming millennium is a matter of increasing conjecture. A baby born this date might have a chance to see what the world is like in 2100.

In recent issues of *The Futurist,* many challenging forecasts have appeared. One frightening prospect based on current fertility rates as projected would put a world population figure of multi-billions by 2150 from the current 5.7 billion. By the year 2000, India may be the second nation in the world (after China) to achieve a population of one billion people. Microwave cooking may be on the way out. In defense of good parenting, one expert claimed society benefits by a million dollars when a child is raised by caring parents, while an incompetently raised child through crime, welfare and other burdens costs society two million dollars. Minority populations in the U.S. will balloon from 24 percent to 47 percent of all Americans by 2050. By 2000 as many as 40 world nations will have the economic and technological potential to become nuclear states.

Also an article by Olesen in the September-October 1995 issue of *The Futurist,* ten technologies were projected with the greatest projection for business profits by 2005. They include:

1. *Genetic mapping*
2. *Super materials*
3. *High-density energy sources*
4. *Digital high-definition television*
5. *Miniaturization technologies*
6. *Smart manufacturing*
7. *Anti-aging products and services*
8. *Medical treatments*

9. Hybrid-fuel vehicles

10. Edutainment

Obviously for a person interested in forecasting future trends, the World Future Society offers an invaluable reference source.

Uncommon Remedies for America's Ills presents an approach to what the future should encompass. In some situations such as finding solutions Y and Z for the baby licensing proposal, technology is leaned on heavily. In most other categories, citizen reaction and activity could bring about a desirable and desired change.

APPENDIX B
INITIATIVE AND REFERENDUM

*T*he Initiative and Referendum are procedures by which voters may express their wishes on matters of government policy or legislation. Each state has a somewhat different approach including varied numbers to gain petition success.

The referendum may be optional or obligatory. Under the latter, a constitution or statute mandates that certain types of legislative enactment be referred to the electors for approval or disapproval. Constitutional amendment proposals by the legislatures of most of the states require a referendum. A specified number of voters may force a popular vote on a specific law enacted by a legislature which enables the voters to countermand the law. This represents an optional referendum. Legislators may also refer issues to the voters to determine the majority opinion (of the voting populace).

The initiative process enables a prescribed number of voters to petition to force a vote on a proposed law or amendment. Initiatives may be direct (when a popular vote is required through petitions) or indirect (when the proposed action is submitted to the legislature). If the legislature fails to take the desired action, then the general voting public can vote on the issue. The legislature may submit an alternative proposal or a statement of why it rejected the proposed action.

The first constitutional referendum in the United States was used by Massachusetts in 1778 toward adopting the United States Constitution. Many examples of the initiative and referendum were used by Switzerland in the 19th century and these models were subsequently adopted by the various united states. Some states require a referendum on bond issues, and local governments often use the obligatory referendum for tax issues, bonds, and related issues. These were developed to enable the citizens to curb political party machines and legislatures which were not responsive to the concerns of the citizenry. The people therefore could override the legislatures and force votes on legislation.

The trend in a number of states is for special interest groups to advance many propositions to the ballot. Often citizens (some states require registered voters living in that district) are paid to solicit signatures on petitions. Usually procuring far more signatures than technically needed is required because some of the people signing are not properly registered voters in the correct district. Signatures must be verified by elections departments. When a large number of propositions appear on the ballot, a strong effort must be made by the voters to be informed on the varied issues. Special interests often spend massive sums to defeat or support issues, often obfuscating the points of the issue to gain an emotional response.

A few of the propositions which have appeared on the ballot for state of California include initiatives against managed health care (June primary 1996), allowing suits on security laws which would counter federal court decisions, tort reform such as no fault insurance (usually backed by insurance companies and opposed by trial lawyer associations), and civil rights issues such as "affirmative action". California voted for term limits, a subject most unpopular with elected officials, and has tackled the immigration issue in recent elections. The subject of dividing California into two or more states periodically rises on the ballot, and after many losses, the lottery finally won on a vote by the people (a questionable victory).

Another issue before a number of states currently is "gay rights". Often when the people react, the courts offset their initiative votes. The citizens of Oregon took on the pensions of state workers and forced employee contributions, only to have this effort offset by the courts.

One of the major issues before the land, certainly not to be enacted voluntarily by the federal congress, is the matter of revising the US Constitution to limit terms of the congressmen.

The point is that eventually the people can react and force the legislature, if not the courts, to modify and even change unpopular laws or develop laws otherwise opposed by the legislators. Reference is made in this book to Howard Jarvis and Paul Gann who took on the state of California and secured the passage of a major tax roll back, the famous Proposition 13. Citizens can make their wishes known!

APPENDIX C

CITIZENS WHO HAVE CHANGED HUMANKIND

*M*y father, Verne Albert McGrew, lived from 1893 to 1978. At times I contemplate how many technological changes took place in his span of life; perhaps more than in any other 85 years in the world's history. When it seems that not that many new things can happen in current lifetimes, we find projections for the coming years that represent ongoing and amazing changes (projected in Appendix A).

A broad overview, perhaps just a scratch of the surface of what transpired between 1893 and 1978 would include modern electric lighting (which became available throughout the United States by the 1930s), the automobile industry, the airplane through the jet age, movies, radio and television, the nuclear era (a mixed blessing), the petroleum industry, a practical telephone system, recording machines through the compact disc, the photocopier, microwave ovens, computers, and man on the moon. These represent but a superficial glimpse of an awesome era.

More than through technological development, our world and our nation have noted impressive social transitions. In this arena, ideas often developed by a single person or a small group of people have made vast, largely positive changes for our society.

One citizen can make a difference!

Think of Rosa Parks whose confrontation with "Jim Crow" laws brought in a modern era of civil rights; the bus ride that altered the history of our nation. Certainly a more powerful leader in the person of Martin Luther King, Jr., whose "dream" inspired his fellow Black Americans, was the catalyst for change. However, actual civil rights laws were placed on the books by the leadership of Lyndon Baines Johnson and Harry Truman. Of course, the door had been opened years before by a man named Abraham Lincoln and the Emancipation Proclamation. Now Jesse Jackson and other black activists continue to strive for understanding and the hearts and consciences of the peoples of our nation.

Environmental protection (as well as auto safety) has been given a major impetus by Ralph Nader in contemporary times, but Teddy Roosevelt, John Muir and a host of others had moved this concept forward earlier in the century.

In the field of education people named Horace Mann and John Dewey have led us into the modern era.

In social welfare Jane Addams and her Hull House development became a model for America.

In the category of religion, distinguished leaders over the centuries have included Martin Luther, Calvin, Knox, and Wesley, and so many who brought religious freedom to North America. In this new land we have seen men such as Joseph Smith and Brigham Young establish a major denomination, The Church of Jesus Christ of the Latter Day Saints, the Mormons. Mary Baker Eddy's vision brought about Christian Science. In contemporary times Dr. Billy Graham has led national crusades throughout America and even the world, while Dr. Robert Schuller brought a television ministry into practically every home in the United States and subsequently to much of the world.

Schuller is an interesting example of one man's making a difference. As an aspiring minister, he was not particularly successful until he and his wife moved to California from the Midwest, and even then he struggled for a few years going door to door in Orange County to encourage people to come to his newly formed church. In fact, the services were held at a drive-in theater, and gradually attendance began to increase. With an inspired thought Schuller invited another major religious figure, Norman Vincent Peale, to preach at his church. To his surprise and delight, Dr. Peale did so which brought thousands into the drive-in church. The congregation was able to buy some land in Garden Grove and ultimately the Crystal Cathedral was created, a major act of faith.

I would be remiss not to mention another amazing man named William Booth who, in 1865, brought about a new organization pledged to work with the commoner who had fallen on hard times. The Salvation Army has impressed me as providing a number of selfless leaders throughout our nation and other parts of the world.

The concept of a League of Nations became a passion with Woodrow Wilson who could not persuade the European leaders to bury their feeling of vengeance against the defeated Germany, nor could he capture the hearts of the American Republican congressional leaders who were pointing inward with a spirit of isolationism . Finally long after Wilson's earthly span, and after the horrors of a second world war in 1945, a renewed effort was made and the United Nations was born.

More ideas? How about Habitat for Humanity which has built an amazing number of low cost homes for Americans of limited means; new homeowners who pledged to give sweat equity to help themselves.

How about the scientists who in barely more than a century have brought modern medicine into being. We think of Fleming, the Curies, and, of course, Jonas Salk and a host of others, practitioners and researchers.

Then there is the written word which informs, entertains, generates thought, stimulates emotions, and promotes ideas and action. The master word craftsman of the English language remains William Shakespeare whose writing is four centuries old and yet ageless.

In our contemporary era, and by using the written word and also the spoken word through the fields of radio and television, we think of such idea and information promulgators as Dr. Joyce Brothers, Ann Landers, Dear Abby, Miss Manners and in the talk show genre such luminaries as Oprah Winfrey and Larry King, and literally a host of other hosts. Even Dr. Ruth Westheimer has popularized and opened up discussion on the timeless, but at one time controversial topic of "sex".

Others whose ideas continue to influence creative people include Alfred Nobel and Joseph Pulitzer. The MacArthur Foundation is supporting creative thinkers and doers on a multitude of scenes with significant financial grants.

Throughout our nation citizens are working hard for their neighborhoods, communities and broader government. George Bush perhaps covered it best in his acceptance address at the Republican Convention:

"We are a nation of communities, of tens and thousands of ethnic, religious, social, business, labor union, neighborhood, regional and other organizations, all of them varied, voluntary and unique...a brilliant diversity spread like stars, like a thousand points of light in a broad and peaceful sky."

When I was a newspaper boy in Iowa, I was inspired by Gardner Cowles, the publisher of the *Des Moines Register and Tribune*. His motto was, "Things don't just happen. Someone makes them happen!" Active citizens can make their neighborhoods a better place. Every person with a few creative ideas and energy to implement them can establish a lasting legacy.

INDEX

BIOGRAPHY

JOHN MCGREW was born in Marshalltown, Iowa. He entered the United States Naval Academy, and graduated in June 1951.

Commissioned as an intelligence officer in the United States Air Force, McGrew served in California, the Philippines, Japan and Korea during the Korean War. He became an administrative assistant to Major General Ernest Moore who served as the Deputy Chief of Staff for Operations under General Mark Clark, Far East Commander.

Returning to the states, McGrew became ill, was hospitalized, and then placed on the temporary disability retired list.

He became an educator and school administrator, eventually becoming a school district superintendent in Sonoma County, California. Upon retiring after a 31 year career, he moved to Ashland, Oregon. McGrew was married and has three children and six grandchildren.

His past community involvement has included establishing a communities scholarship association, holding various offices in the church, charter president of the Sonoma County Association of School Administrators, past president of a Rotary club, past president of the Analy Community Concert Association, past president of the Western Sonoma County Historical Society, past president of the Sonoma County Museum, Chairman of a Bicentennial Commission, and past president of a TROA chapter. He is a life member of the United States Naval Academy Alumni Association, and a member of the World Future Society.

McGrew has written extensively for various educational magazines, the *Los Angeles Times, Glendora Press, Santa Rosa Press Democrat* and other papers. He has published one book, *Navigating Career Change*. He unsuccessfully ran for Congress in Orange County, California. McGrew received the American Educator's Medal from the Freedom's Foundation, and was a fellow with the National Academy of School Executives. He developed and appeared in an educational TV series for Los Angeles County schools.

McGrew received his masters degree at Long Beach State and his doctorate at the University of Southern California. Additional graduate work was taken at the Claremont Graduate School, the College for Financial Planning, University of California at Berkeley and Santa Barbara, the University of Wisconsin, Columbia University and Harvard University.